ORIGINAL WRITING

'A brilliant series – an absolute gift for teachers! This superb series makes clear tangible terminology and implicit meanings which to many students seem foreign. The books' methods and tactics are enjoyable and workable for both students and teachers, and the clear, evaluative and reflective models will enable students to obtain the necessary reflection in their own written responses.'

> Kesner Ridge, Hagley Roman Catholic High School, Worcestershire, and Outstanding New Teacher 2002 (*The Guardian Teaching Awards*)

'This is the series we've all been waiting for! Tightly focused on the assessment objectives, these books provide an excellent aid to classroom teaching and self-study. Whether your school changes board or text, or decides to offer Literature and/or Language to 6th formers these books are still the tool that can make a real difference to results.'

> Emmeline McChleery, Aylesford School, Warwick

Routledge A Level English Guides equip AS and A2 Level students with the skills they need to explore, evaluate, and enjoy English. What has – until now – been lacking for the revised English A Levels is a set of textbooks that equip students with the concepts, skills and knowledge they need to succeed in light of the way the exams are actually working. The *Routledge A Level English Guides* series fills this critical gap.

Books in the series are built around the various skills specified in the assessment objectives (AOs) for all AS and A2 Level English courses, and take into account how these AOs are being interpreted by the exam boards. Focusing on the AOs most relevant to their topic, the books help students to develop their knowledge and abilities through analysis of a wide range of texts and data. Each book also offers accessible **explanations**, **examples**, **exercises**, **summaries**, **suggested answers** and a **glossary of key terms**.

The series helps students to learn what is required of them and develop skills accordingly, while ensuring that English remains an exciting subject that students enjoy studying. The books are also an essential resource for teachers trying to create lessons which balance the demands of the exam boards with the more general skills and knowledge students need for the critical appreciation of English Language and Literature.

ROUTLEDGE A LEVEL ENGLISH GUIDES

About the Series Editor

Adrian Beard was Head of English at Gosforth High School, Newcastle upon Tyne. He now works at the University of Newcastle upon Tyne and is a Chief Examiner for AS and A2 Level English Literature. He is co-series editor of the Routledge Intertext series, and his publications include *Texts and Contexts*, *The Language of Politics*, and *The Language of Sport* (all for Routledge).

TITLES IN THE SERIES

The Language of Literature
Adrian Beard

How Texts Work
Adrian Beard

Language and Social Contexts
Amanda Coultas

Writing for Assessment
Angela Goddard

Original Writing
Sue Morkane

Transforming Texts
Shaun O'Toole

Texts through History
Adele Wills

ORIGINAL WRITING

Sue Morkane

LONDON AND NEW YORK

First published 2004 by Routledge
11 New Fetter Lane, London EC4P 4EE

Simultaneously published in the USA and Canada
by Routledge
29 West 35th Street, New York, NY 10001

Routledge is an imprint of the Taylor & Francis Group

© 2004 Sue Morkane

Typeset in Galliard by Keystroke, Jacaranda Lodge, Wolverhampton
Printed and bound in Great Britain by TJ International Ltd, Padstow, Cornwall

All rights reserved. No part of this book may be reprinted or reproduced
or utilised in any form or by any electronic, mechanical, or other means,
now known or hereafter invented, including photocopying and recording,
or in any information storage or retrieval system, without permission in
writing from the publishers.

British Library Cataloguing in Publication Data
A catalogue record for this book is available from the British Library

Library of Congress Cataloging in Publication Data
Morkane, Sue, 1950–
  Original writing / Sue Morkane.
    (Paperback : alk. paper) p. cm. – (Routledge A level English guides)
  1. English language–Rhetoric. 2. Report writing. I. Title. II. Series.
PE1408 .M693 2004
808'. 042–dc22   2003018037

ISBN 0–415–31911–0 (hbk)
ISBN 0–415–31912–9 (pbk)

CONTENTS

List of illustrations   vii
Preface   ix
Acknowledgements   xiii

1 The Commentary   1
   Some of the best writing breaks the rules 1
   Why do you have to write a commentary? 1
   That initial inspiration 2
   Doing the background research 2
   Designing your text 3
   Identifying the significant features 3
   Drafts and redrafts 4
   Audience feedback 7
   Differentiation 7
   The style model 7
   Putting it all together 8

2 Writing to Entertain – the Short Story   13
   Introduction 13
   Finding your voice 13
   The structure 14
   Beginnings 16
   Point of view 18
   Showing, not telling 19
   The effectiveness of humour 21
   Writing to entertain – other ideas 21

3 Writing to Entertain – Spoken Texts   27
   Introduction 27
   The dramatic monologue 27
   Sketch writing 31
   Radio, television, play and film scripts 33
   And now for some ideas for plots 39

4 Writing to Inform   41
Introduction 41
The personal voice 41
The public voice – investigation and public information 50

5 Writing to Instruct and Advise   57
Introduction 57
Think of your audience 57
What are the features of an instructive text? 63
How to make it interesting . . . 63
More advice than instruction . . . 64
And finally, some advice from aunty 67

6 Voicing Argument: the Art of Persuasion   71
Introduction 71
Friends, Romans, countrymen . . . persuasive speech 71
Persuasion in print 77
The issue of plagiarism 79

7 How to Get Started   83

Suggestions for answer   87
Glossary   89

ILLUSTRATIONS

FIGURES

1.1	'Hard Times for Magwitch's Marsh'	10
4.1	'The Star Spangles' by Jane Gillow	48
4.2	'Drugs and Solvents: A Young Person's Guide'	52
4.3	'The Score: Facts About Drugs'	53
5.1	'Revision Blues?' study guide	61–2
5.2	'What do you think you are looking at?'	65
5.3	'Love S.T.I.NGS'	66
7.1	*Driveon* Contents page, 2003	84

TABLE

5.1	Comparison of radiotherapy passages 1 and 2	59

PREFACE

This book has two very simple aims: (1) to help you to write, and (2) to help you to enjoy the writing process. Of course, if you are using this book in order to fulfil the requirements of A Level English language or English language and literature, then you must also be aware of the specifications for the original writing component of these subjects.

ASSESSMENT OBJECTIVES

The AS/A2 specifications in English are governed by assessment objectives (or AOs) which break down each of the subjects into component parts and skills. These assessment objectives have been used to create the different modules which together form a sort of jigsaw puzzle. Different objectives are highlighted in different modules, but at the end of AS and again at the end of A2 each of the objectives has been given a roughly equal weighting.

The ideas and activities in this book will relate most closely to the following assessment objectives:

English Language

AO1: you must be able to communicate clearly your knowledge about language, using correct terms and writing with accuracy and fluency

AO2: you must show your own expertise and accuracy in writing for a variety of different purposes and audiences, using linguistic features to explain and comment on the choices you have made

AO4: your accompanying commentary must show that you can understand, discuss and explore the way language is used in everyday contexts

---

> **English Language and Literature**
>
> **AO3**: you must use and evaluate different literary and linguistic approaches to the study of written and spoken language, showing how these approaches inform your reading
>
> **AO4**: in your commentary you are expected to show that you understand the ways in which context, form, style and vocabulary shape the ways meanings can be found in texts
>
> **AO6**: you must show your expertise and accuracy in writing for a variety of specific purposes and audiences, drawing on your knowledge of literary texts and features of language

HOW CAN YOU USE THIS BOOK?

The format of this book consists of chapters which focus on the different purposes you may write for: that is, entertainment, information, instruction/advice and persuasion. Within these there is differentiation between texts that are designed to be spoken and those that are written. However, many texts don't fit readily into a neat classification by purpose, so you must not look at one chapter and think that you are limited by the forms given as examples within it.

For example, look at what the specification for one board outlined as suggestions for coursework topics, and you will see that many of the suggested forms could be used for different purposes:

- Writing to entertain
  - a short story
  - a stand-up comedy routine
  - a radio script
- Writing to persuade
  - a piece of journalism
  - a moral fable
  - texts for an advertising campaign
- Writing to inform
  - an account of an event
  - an explanation of a process
  - an article about an area of special interest
- Writing to advise/instruct
  - planning for an event or occasion
  - making better use of computer software
  - advice on managing money

The narrative approach you take for a short story could equally be used for an informative travelogue or a persuasive spoken message to a school assembly. Your piece of journalism could be fact-based, investigative and objective; in other words, informative, rather than being subjective, emotive and persuasive. An explanation of a process might be part of a scripted radio talk, or a 'how to' instruction guide. Many of the best texts use unusual and imaginative forms to engage their readers.

All the forms of writing suggested can be (and have been) accomplished successfully by students. However, right from the outset it is important to stress that you should choose tasks which reflect your own interests and for which you perceive a *real* audience.

Each chapter contains a number of exercises, a few testing your knowledge but the majority suggesting practical writing tasks. When the exercise introduces a new idea, there will be suggestions for an answer immediately following. When the exercise checks to see if a point has been understood, suggestions for answer may be found at the back of the book.

ACKNOWLEDGEMENTS

Thanks to: Beth Webb, Somerset author, Mike James, News Editor of Minster FM, and Phil Bird, songwriter, musician and visual artist, for kindly giving me permission to use their advice to A Level students.

Debbie Rundle, editor, and Matthew Chorley, reporter, for the *Taunton Times*, for their advice and expertise on journalistic matters.

My grateful thanks to the following students for permission to use their work: Jake Ellwood; Alexa Lymer; Lee Matthews; Sarah Hunt; Sara Reimers; Thomas Hawkins; Hugh Wright; James Beal; Nicholas Randall; Richard Tunley; Louise Hawkins; Kate Mulcahy; Karen Thompson.

The author would like to thank the following copyright holders: Rosemary Horstmann, 'Drama on the Air', in *Writing for Radio*, 'Writing Handbooks' series (A&C Black, 1997).

Extract from *Talking Heads* by Alan Bennett, reproduced by permission of BBC Worldwide Limited. Copyright © Alan Bennett 1988.

Extract from *Harry Enfield and his Humorous Chums* by Harry Enfield (Penguin, 1997), reproduced by permission of Penguin Books Limited. Copyright © Harry Enfield.

Extract from *The Office: The Scripts, Series 1* by Ricky Gervais and Steve Merchant (BBC Consumer Publishing, 2002). Reproduced by permission of PFD.

Extract from 'The Star Spangles' by Jane Gillow from *Kerrang!*, 12 April 2003, reproduced by permission of Emap Performance.

Extract from 'Radcliffe's Brave Feats Leave her Walking on Air' by Simon Barnes from *The Times*, 14 April 2003. Reproduced by permission of News International Syndication.

'Mills and Boon Discover the Mini-Saga or Love Among the Laundry' reproduced by permission of the *Sunday Telegraph*.

'Drugs and Solvents: A Young Person's Guide' and 'The Score: Facts About Drugs', reproduced by permission of Crown Copyright.

'What do you think you're looking at?', leaflet reproduced by permission of *mentality*.

'Love S.T.I.NGS', reproduced by kind permission of fpa from *Love S.T.I.NGS: A Beginner's Guide to Sexually Transmitted Infections*. Copyright © fpa 1999. Created for fpa by Comic Company. Illustrations by Ed Hillyer.

Contents page from *DriveOn*, 2003, reproduced by permission of the Driving Standards Agency.

Mexican Chilli Con Carnage, reprinted by permission of Amnesty International.

THE COMMENTARY   CHAPTER 1

SOME OF THE BEST WRITING BREAKS THE RULES

Why *start* a book about writing with the commentary? This is an exercise that most students see as the final process. You will not find an English language or an English language and literature specification which begins with the commentary; rather, it begins with the writing process. The task of the commentary is to illuminate this process of writing from the point of view of you, the writer. So asking you to start at the end may seem a strange, even illogical suggestion. After all, how can you comment on something that you have not yet written?

However, just as some of the best writing deliberately flouts the rules, so 'starting at the end' will be very helpful to you as a writer. Writing is a *process* and you must be aware at all stages of your writing of the reasons for your language choices. If you regard the commentary as a bolt-on exercise in which you treat your own writing as distanced from yourself and on which you perform the sort of stylistics exercise you do for other parts of the course, you will have missed a most important feature: the relationship between yourself as *producer* and the text that you finally produce. If you are self-aware you will be constantly asking yourself:

- Is what I am writing appropriate for my chosen audience?
- Do I need to do more research into this area?
- Have I listened to what my target audience have said?

If you keep answering these questions, you will be constructively self-critical from the start.

WHY DO YOU HAVE TO WRITE A COMMENTARY?

Commentary writing not only makes you think about the choices you have made as a writer, but it is your chance to show your reader (in this case the examiner) just how conscious those decisions were. A good commentary can shed light on an experimental piece of writing; for example, helping the reader to understand what you are trying to do.

However, your writing does not have to be ground-breaking in any way to benefit from the skills which a commentary encourages. These skills include the need to:

- show awareness of the ways in which texts achieve their purpose
- redraft and listen to advice
- evaluate what you have written

The commentary serves a further purpose if you are writing for coursework; it provides a safeguard against **plagiarism**.

The length of the commentary differs depending on which board you are writing for, but all boards require you to take the following points into consideration.

THAT INITIAL INSPIRATION

First of all, what are the *origins* of your piece of writing? You may have been inspired to write a short story or play script by a song or book title, catchy phrase or unusual **collocation**. A quirky or moving news item may have been the stimulus for a different genre or purpose.

Personal interest is most important. First-hand experience of, for example, bullying or body image problems can come alive on the page. It is then easy to write about your role as producer of that text, your purpose in writing it and its intended effect on a particular audience.

DOING THE BACKGROUND RESEARCH

To write with conviction you must know your facts. The commentary allows you to demonstrate the research that you have undertaken. More will be said about this when looking at the importance of good style models at the end of this chapter, but if you are writing to inform, instruct or persuade, the facts and figures which you download from the Internet, take from an encyclopaedia or transcribe from the words of an expert give your work credibility and convince your chosen audience. Another reason for regarding your commentary as a first step in the writing process is to remind yourself of the importance of planning. You will save valuable time if you record the name, author, publisher (if relevant), date and page reference (again if relevant) of any piece of information you may wish to refer to again. If you need to write to an organisation to request information this still takes time, even in the age of the email and fax.

(See the companion volume in this series, *Writing for Assessment* by Angela Goddard, for further advice on sourcing and referencing.)

DESIGNING YOUR TEXT

Nor is it only the content of the piece you have written that may require research. How suitable is your writing for its chosen format? Do you, for example, know the differences between a broadsheet and a tabloid newspaper? (In a recent survey of a language group beginning their AS course, a majority defined these in terms of size of newspaper, with far fewer mentioning content, **register**, **tone** or stylistic features.) Can you distinguish between newspapers of the same broad type?

Consider the appropriateness of the following extract from the opening paragraph of a commentary written in a recent original writing exam to accompany an entertaining feature article for the weekend magazine supplement of a national broadsheet newspaper. The article (not reproduced here) had to be based on people's experience of part-time work. The candidate amusingly used the **semantic fields** of horror and hell: the owner of the restaurant where he worked became the 'Queen of the Damned', the hotel itself the 'Dante Arms'. (The candidate assumed that his audience would know that Dante was the Italian poet whose *Inferno* describes a journey through Hell.)

> The text of the article 'Saturday in Hell's Kitchen' has been written for an audience of adults, possibly younger adults, who favour the more subversive, ironic humour that can frequently be seen in *The Times* or the *Guardian*. The function of the article is to entertain, largely through humour . . . especially the friendly and informal style used in Saturday magazine supplements, e.g. Will Self's humorous column in *The Times*.

Not only is the writer conscious of the **genre** for which he is writing – broadsheet newspapers – he can also name appropriate examples: *The Times* and the *Guardian*. He is also suitably tentative in his claims: *possibly* younger adults.

IDENTIFYING THE SIGNIFICANT FEATURES

You must also identify the significant features in your writing that show you are aware of the genre you have chosen. The writer of 'Hell's Kitchen', for example, is clear in his intentions:

> I have followed the format of the newspaper feature article to the extent that there is a title, and a leading passage to introduce the author and the article, using another journalistic device, a piece in parentheses, to lead into the main body of the text.

The following chapters of this book will concentrate on detailing the features of different genres.

At this point it is important to note that you must concentrate on the question 'How do the features that I have highlighted work in their genre?' rather than simply asking yourself 'What are the features?' and working through a checklist. Avoid the obvious ('My text contains a mixture of simple and complex sentences' is a statement that would apply to virtually all texts), the merely descriptive ('I have used alliteration') and using terminology simply for the sake of it.

The Point of View

It is important that you comment on the appropriateness of the **point of view** which you have adopted. The point of view, or stance that you take as a writer, will be discussed in detail in Chapter 2. You must remember that you establish the tone and mood of your piece by the way in which, for example, you address your reader. I have chosen to address you in this book directly by using the **pronoun** 'you' because this book is essentially a practical guide in which I share with you tips and experience from years of teaching. Sharing is an inclusive activity, which invites a tone that is less formal and more relaxed. Had I addressed this text to 'the student' or 'the candidate' I would have made it impersonal and distanced myself from you, the reader. There is nothing wrong with distance – it just depends on what you are trying to achieve with a text. So, to sum up, the choices we make as writers often have complex social and cultural implications attached.

DRAFTS AND REDRAFTS

One of the most important features of the commentary is your recognition of the changes you have made to your writing, especially if you have to submit evidence of drafting and revisions. Even when you have written under exam conditions you are expected to comment on improvements you could make. Since most students word process even their first draft for coursework, it can be very difficult to see what alterations have been made. Always number your drafts clearly and get into the habit of highlighting the changes you have made, perhaps by italicising or underlining them (the Track Changes tool in word-processing packages offers another way of doing this). Then when you write your commentary you will be reminded that you made a change and will be able to comment on it.

There are two reasons why commenting on the drafting process is so important:

1. Writing a text is an evolving process and if you are being self-critical you will find more appropriate lexical choices, omit some writing altogether and occasionally alter your sentence structure.
2. You provide a safeguard against any question of plagiarism.

Exercise 1

One way to demonstrate how writing a text is an evolving process is to study the differences in the drafts made by a published writer.

The following are two versions of a poem by Wilfred Owen. 'Last Words' is a draft, and 'The Last Laugh' is the final version.

- What changes has Owen made from draft to final version?
- Why do you think he made them?

Set out your findings in columns, noting the changes that have been made. You may find it helpful to explore the differences in terms of **semantics**, **grammar**, **phonology** and **syntax**.

Last Words

'O Jesus Christ!' one fellow sighed
And kneeled and bowed, tho' not in prayer, and died.
And the Bullets sang 'In vain!',
Machine-guns chuckled 'Vain!',
Big Guns guffawed 'In vain!'

'Father and Mother!' one boy said.
Then smiled – at nothing, like a small child, being dead.
And the Shrapnel Cloud
Slowly gestured 'Vain',
The falling Splinters muttered 'Vain'.

'My love!' another cried, 'My love, my bud'.
Then, gently lowered, his whole face kissed the mud.
And the flares gesticulated 'Vain',
The Shells hooted 'In vain',
And the Gas hissed 'In vain'.

The Last Laugh

'O Jesus Christ! I'm hit!' he said, and died.
Whether he vainly cursed, or prayed indeed,
The bullets chirped – In vain! vain! vain!
Machine-guns chuckled – Tut-tut! Tut-tut!
And the Big Gun guffawed.

continued

> Another sighed – 'O Mother, mother! Dad!'
> Then smiled at nothing, childlike, being dead.
> And the lofty Shrapnel-cloud
> Leisurely gestured – Fool!
> And the falling splinters tittered.
>
> 'My love!' one moaned. Love-languid seemed his mood,
> Till, slowly lowered, his whole face kissed the mud.
> And the Bayonets' long teeth grinned;
> Rabbles of Shells hooted and groaned;
> And the Gas hissed.

Suggestions for Answer

Notice that the verbs in both versions focus on the semantic field of laughter, but whereas 'chuckled' and 'guffawed' are found in both, the laughter in 'The Last Laugh' has more of a mocking edge. 'Muttered' becomes 'tittered', the bayonets' long teeth 'grinned' and the shells both 'hooted' and 'groaned'.

Grammatically, there is a subtle difference in meaning between 'And the Gas hissed "In vain"' and 'The Gas hissed'. Both might be interpreted as the gas making a noise of disapproval but the final version could also indicate something more ominous: the sound made by poison gas as it is released from its pressurised container.

Notice how subtle the phonological changes are as well. The sibilant 's' is more pronounced in 'gas hissed' than when the shape of the mouth and tongue is changing to accommodate 'in vain' and the syntax (these are the final two words of the poem) gives added impact. Notice too the use of **onomatopoeia** in mimicking the staccato sound of the machine-guns – 'Tut-tut! Tut-tut'! – and the whine of the bullets – 'In vain! vain! vain!' Even the half rhymes 'Dad/dead', 'mood/mud', instead of the more romantic and conventional 'said/dead', 'bud/mud', capture the sense of dissonance that Owen is trying to present.

The contrast between the association of verbs such as 'chirp' (bird sound), 'guffaw' (boisterous laugh) and 'chuckle' (quiet laugh) with pleasant activities and the actual situation gives 'The Last Laugh' its bite. It is the weaponry that is having the 'last laugh'.

Owen's point that war is futile is made in both versions, but is more dramatic and the **irony** sharper in 'The Last Laugh'. There is more mockery and derision in adding the adjective 'lofty' to 'the Shrapnel-cloud' and changing the adverb 'slowly' to 'leisurely'. Both semantically and phonologically Owen is emphasising the fact that it is the weapons of war that are in control.

As you can see from the above, relatively few changes were needed to portray the message more powerfully.

The second reason for commenting on the drafts you have made is the opportunity it gives you to prove 'ownership' of a text. This is an area of concern to many markers of coursework. How can you show that a well-written instruction leaflet or a public service notice is your own authentic work and has not been plagiarised from someone else's text? Always include a hard copy of the material that you have downloaded from websites or photocopies from books and journals you have used as sources of information. You can then demonstrate the ways in which you have created a new text from it. See Chapter 6 for a student's commentary on a charity mailshot, showing how he avoided 'copy-shadowing'.

AUDIENCE FEEDBACK

It is essential to keep your chosen audience in mind if you are to write appropriately and effectively. It may seem obvious if you are doing a coursework task to test it on the audience you are writing for, and bring the findings into your commentary, but surprisingly few students do this meaningfully. The complacent 'my audience really liked it' convinces nobody.

DIFFERENTIATION

This chapter has stressed the importance of being clear about the audience you are writing for, the genre and the purpose. Identify each of these carefully in your commentary. Some examination boards require you to write two pieces for different audiences and purposes and in different genres. This again requires careful planning. For example, you may decide that you want your first piece to be an autobiographical short story for a teenage audience. You cannot then write a leaflet for teenagers warning about the dangers of drugs, without being accused of writing for the same audience. Writing for a 'general' or 'mass' audience, on the other hand, encourages unfocused writing and even vaguer commentaries.

If you do have to produce a folder which demonstrates a variety of writing for different audiences, purposes and genres, it is good practice to note in the top corner of your very first draft (and every subsequent draft) what these are. You will then be reminded of the requirements, and will not fall into the trap of writing for the same audience or using the same form in your second piece.

THE STYLE MODEL

A style model is simply an example belonging to the same genre as the piece for which you have written. Distinctive features used by experienced writers in that field may be identified and commented on in your commentary (if word limit allows). If you are writing a **dramatic monologue**, for example, you may well find it useful to look at Alan Bennett's *Talking Heads*.

It can also be very useful for your examiner to have an authentic version of, say, a music review from *NME*, or a feature article from *More!*, both examples aimed at a younger age group. Even more important is the need to give examples of fanzines and material, especially **satire**, that you have downloaded from websites and which may not be widely known. Follow and adapt the style and layout of the *best* writing you can find in the field for which you are writing.

PUTTING IT ALL TOGETHER

To finish this chapter here is the full commentary from a piece of coursework which won a national competition seeking a feature article on the theme *One Landscape, Many Views*. The first page of three of the student's article is also included, but not his style model and his letters to the RSPB, British Airways and local residents, nor their very full replies in response. (In all, there were sixteen pages of evidence and research.)

Commentary: 'Hard Times For Magwitch's Marsh'

The purpose of 'Hard Times for Magwitch's Marsh' is to inform the reader about negative aspects of building an airport at Cliffe Marshes, north Kent. The genre is for a feature article in an environmental issues magazine and therefore the audience is slanted at anybody with an interest in the environment. For display purposes I have named the magazine *EnvironmentEye* and I have presented the piece in its published form, as the presentational devices are key to attracting the reader's attention to and understanding of the topic.

The discourse of the article has been specifically structured to include the main arguments from a mass of information that shows many different views. The subject is introduced with a description of the area and what the proposals are, and as the environmental impacts are by far the largest concern for the area, the RSPB's view is represented first. The social impact (shown by the local resident's view) and the practical difficulties of building an airport at Cliffe are described after this. The view of the RCEP is particularly important, as it is a Government commission opposing Government plans. The article is ended with an emotive passage that touches on how an issue like this affects the reader. The use of facts (the statistics) juxtapositioned around the author's opinions is a method of disguising the highly opinionated approach of the article so the reader follows the author's view (influential power).

As this is a formal article for a formal publication the lexis is relatively high-order. Specific use of the pronoun 'you' in the second paragraph immediately gets the reader involved in the issue. Much of the lexis throughout is intentionally emotive to get the reader's support for the 'No Airport At Cliffe' campaign. Adjectives such as 'destroyed' and 'fierce', intensifiers such as 'extremely' and the emotive noun 'tragedy' all work to this effect. Specific parts of the quotations I obtained from my sources were chosen specially to include the most emotive expressions.

There are several reasons why there is variation in the sentence structure. Long and complex sentences give the impression of an educated approach which in turn creates a desire on the reader's part to take the subject seriously. However, the use of simple declaratives at the same time, such as 'The marshes are a mysterious place', make the article slightly more personal and informal.

Many features of language are used to create a positive reaction from the reader. The double intertextuality with Dickens' novel *Hard Times* and Magwitch, the character from *Great Expectations*, as well as the alliteration in the title 'Hard Times For Magwitch's Marsh' immediately has the effect a title needs to get the reader interested in reading the article. There is a *double entendre* in the byline; the word 'explores' not only refers to the proposals but also makes a connection with the marsh itself. There is another play on words with the connection between birds arriving at the marsh and the landing of planes at an airport. Throughout there is a negative evaluation of the Government and negative words are used in association with them, for example, 'ignore' and 'yet still'. Again this has influential power over the audience and leads the reader to accept that the author's view is the correct one. The final statement is blunt and widens the issue: 'There wouldn't be any part of the UK that couldn't be redecorated with concrete.' The conclusion is the final point so it is important that the reader goes away thinking about the issue.

I wrote to the RSPB, BA and the local council in order to make the article as accurate as possible. I have also chosen one main style model, an article published in the RSPB's magazine, *Birds*. This shows some of the presentational devices that are important for attracting the reader which I have adopted, such as the use of images. As it is in an environmental magazine itself it was useful to refer to when deciding how my views should be voiced in my article. The author has also started his article with a description of the area he discusses.

I have made several changes between the first and final draft. I altered the way in which the different views were introduced, for example, '"We are deeply saddened," says Chris Corrigan', rather than, 'the RSPB has said . . .'. Another important change I made was with the presentation so that the genre as a feature was more established with the inclusion of images, a pull-quote, a byline and titles, as well as a box containing links for further information.

EnvironmentEye

Hard Times For Magwitch's Marsh

Hugh Wright explores the plans to destroy Cliffe Marshes.

Cliffe Marshes and the Thames Estuary.

ONE hundred and forty-two years after 'Great Expectations' was first published, the setting Dickens described as a 'dark flat wilderness' still remains the same, wonderfully untouched state that it was then. The marshes at Cliffe in north Kent are an extensive area of wet meadow habitat with saline pools and ancient ditches that are a haven for wildlife, particularly migratory birds. Though how long the marshes stay a wilderness is in question this year, as plans to build a four-runway airport have been put forward by the Department for Transport.

The marshes are a mysterious place. Whilst you feel you are in a desolate and deserted landscape, bright lights shine at you from the large industries on the surrounding banks of the Thames. A ship may crawl slowly along the horizon and planes fly overhead. The area is only thirty miles from the centre of London and yet it seems one of the wildest places you may ever visit.

Around one hundred and fifty-five thousand visitors fly in to Cliffe each year, when many species of waterfowl arrive to spend the winter there. Cliffe is already an international airport, with connections to Greenland and Siberia along the migration routes of some of the birds. However metal-winged flyers could be landing at Cliffe bringing in 58 million passengers, as early as 2015.

It is estimated that there will be a 60% increase in the number of air passengers between 2000 and 2030, reaching 500 million people a year, 300 million of whom are expected to travel in the South East. In a simple 'predict and provide' policy, the Government has proposed to increase airport capacity in the South East and a brand new airport at Cliffe is one of the options.

The Government would like to see a site that could connect national and international flights - a 'hub' airport. The development would be so large that 2,600 hectares of land would be destroyed to accommodate it, that's twice the size of Heathrow today.

> "To destroy a site so precious is an act of pure vandalism"

The Government believes the land at Cliffe is suitable for an airport because it will avoid creating noise pollution over London; good transport links can be made; twenty-four hour operation can take place and it could trigger regeneration in the Thames Gateway.

The RSPB has shown fierce opposition to the plans as the charity manages six areas of land that would be damaged or destroyed by the airport.

Figure 1.1 'Hard Times for Magwitch's Marsh'

SUMMARY

In this chapter you have explored:

- The importance of considering writing as an evolving process, in which you must be aware of the reasons for your language choices
- The way personal interest and informed choice (in particular, research) helps you to write well
- The need for an analytical approach: identifying the significant features in a text to demonstrate awareness of the genre and the point of view adopted
- The importance of drafting to demonstrate the improvements you have made and to authenticate the text as your own work
- The relationship, not only between producer and text, but also between producer and receiver: the importance of getting feedback from your chosen audience
- The need to demonstrate awareness of the different audiences and purposes for which you are writing and the different genres chosen

WRITING TO ENTERTAIN – THE SHORT STORY

CHAPTER 2

INTRODUCTION

Writing a short story is a very popular choice for students. The best of these are superb, and worthy of wider publication. However, short story writing requires careful thought and planning if you are to be successful. In particular, watch the 'relentlessly chronological' autobiographical short story, which typically has features such as the following:

> At 7.30 there was a ring on the doorbell. It was Ali and Chris. We started to get ready for the big night out. At 8.00, after a drink or two to get us into the mood, there was a rush for the mirror in the bathroom for those final touches. We had booked a taxi for 8.30 and it duly arrived.

To avoid recounting (in the words of Mark Twain) 'one damned thing after another', you must pay careful attention to the craft of storytelling. After all, your intention is to *entertain*.

FINDING YOUR VOICE

In a recent forum for would-be writers on Radio 5 Live the question was asked: 'What is the most important thing to keep in mind if you want to be a successful writer?' The answer was: 'Find your voice.' This means writing from within, developing your own individual voice and having the confidence to tell a story your way.

First of all, choose a subject area that you are interested in and know something about. This may sound obvious, but your reader will detect immediately if you are half-heartedly rehashing the storyline of one of the soaps or the detective story you watched on television last week. This is not telling it honestly your way. There are no short cuts. Your story does not become 'interesting' because it is set in New York or Bali (unless of course you have first-hand experience of either), and focusing on 'universal' themes such as tragedy, disaster or war tends to lead to stories which are melodramatic and unconvincing. The best writing has a real sense of *interest* and *engagement* with the task.

THE STRUCTURE

Having chosen your topic, think carefully about how you are going to structure your narrative.

Traditionally, a narrative structure falls into four parts:

- The *introduction* or exposition, in which you establish your characters, the setting and the context in which they find themselves
- The *complication*, in which you introduce a problem
- The *climax*, the 'high point' on which all the action has centred so far
- The *resolution*, in which you bring events to a conclusion

This structure has a number of advantages. Whether you are writing for coursework or an exam you will have a restriction on the number of words you can use. Having a tight framework will give you discipline. You can make every detail count and it will help give you a sense of *shape*.

Of course there are other **discourse structures** you may use. The detective story (and sometimes the mystery and horror as well) may well start with the dead body (or its gruesome discovery) and then go back to the start in order to build in the clues that will enable the reader to reconstruct what has happened. Whatever you choose, your reader is looking for you to shape a satisfying storyline with perhaps a moral, a reversal, a twist, a solution or at least an outcome of some kind.

Making sure your text has a clear, overall structure means that you must be careful with formats such as diary entries, letters or text messages. Many students capture the easy, spontaneous style of these forms with success, but find it much harder to craft their text for *effect*. For the same reason be careful if you are adopting the style of writing known as **stream of consciousness**. The term refers to the stream of impressions, perceptions and thoughts which flow unbidden through our minds. Unfortunately the popularity of this style means that many students treat it as an easy shorthand which is too often random and illogical.

However, the only format that really is off limits is the opening to a novel. You cannot set up a complicated plot and simply leave it to the reader's imagination how it will be resolved. Nor can you develop your characters in a genre whose scale is so much vaster. The reader is left wondering how to make sense of what is only a fragment of the narrative. Again the question has to be asked: Is this entertaining?

Exercise 1

Read the following text from *The Book of Mini-Sagas*. It is one of a collection of mini-sagas from a competition run by the *Sunday Telegraph Magazine*. The rules of the competition stated that the mini-saga had to be written in fifty words. Of course, you will not be asked to write a narrative within such a formal constraint, but the structural and stylistic considerations that you yourself will need to make are here in a very concentrated form.

- Comment on the narrative structure
- What features are used to make this interesting for the reader?

> **MILLS AND BOON DISCOVER THE MINI-SAGA OR LOVE AMONG THE LAUNDRY**
>
> When Sally found a man's striped sock curled among her clothes at the launderette she returned it to the tall dark young man with a shy smile. They met there every week for several months, then were seen no more. One of their wedding presents had been a washing machine.
>
> Reproduced by permission of the *Sunday Telegraph*

Suggestions for Answer

Despite its brevity, the narrative has a **traditional structure**; the characters and the context in which they find themselves are set out clearly for the reader in the introduction. The complication and climax coincide in the statement that the characters 'were seen no more'. The twist in the final line resolves the conflict: the pair have married and do not need to use the launderette any more as they have their own washing machine.

The narrative relies on the audience recognising a number of allusions to other genres. The capitalisation and **alliteration** (Love among the Laundry) is a feature of tabloid newspaper headlines. The popular romance genre is characterised not only by the reference to Mills and Boon but also the cliché 'tall dark young man' and the suggestive 'curled'. The enjoyment you get from reading this story relies on your realising what the implicit meanings are in the lexical detail.

BEGINNINGS

Nothing is more important than the opening. Engage your reader from the start and they will read your text with interest. Begin with the title. Consider **intertextuality**, such as 'To Be or Not to Be . . . in Torquay When the Surf's Up', a **pun**: 'Fission Chips' (a romance which blossoms in the unlikely setting of a visit to a nuclear power-station) or an apparent **contradiction**: 'The Next Train Has Gone Ten Minutes Ago'. These three titles were chosen by students to create interest and curiosity.

There are a number of different ways to make an impact in your opening. You might create an appropriate setting. Dialogue immediately plunges your reader into the action. You may also consider a more self-consciously crafted opening, with a quotation, witty saying, or another dramatic device. (See Text B below, where the student used Victorian novelist John Meade Falkner as an inspiration. Falkner had a fascination with word games.)

Other effective openings involve building up suspense. Charles Dickens indicates the unusual in his short story 'The Signalman': 'instead of looking up to where I stood . . . he turned himself about and looked down the line. There was something remarkable in his manner of doing so.' Edgar Allan Poe's 'The Pit and the Pendulum' builds on a sense of anticipation and horror: 'I was sick – sick unto death.' Finally, you might start in the middle of the action. The technical name for this is starting **in medias res**. However, it is a technique that needs to be treated with care. Katherine Mansfield captures the rather gushy, confidential tone of her narrator in 'The Garden Party', with the simple device of starting her story with a co-ordinating conjunction 'and': 'And after all the weather was ideal. They could not have had a more perfect day for a garden-party if they had ordered it.'

You will notice that references have been made here to the writing of established authors. The more you read a range of good models, the better your own writing will become.

Exercise 2

Consider the following student responses to the title 'Fresh Starts' and the techniques used to engage the reader in these three openings. Then write your own opening to the same title: 'Fresh Starts'.

There are no suggestions for answer to this exercise.

Text A

It wasn't just the presence of tourists and seagulls that made it seem like a different country; there was an indescribable feeling in the air, a taste of salty contentment that seemed to seep into every corner of the town.

Even the supermarkets were full of freckled and sandy children and masculine blonde shop assistants earning their beer money. The streets were slow moving and of the few cars that passed, all were laden with surfboards and starry-eyed teenagers travelling uphill towards the beach. In a few hours the Headland car park would be full. However at this time in the morning it seemed that the whole population of the town was squashed into CJ's All Day Breakfasts, where Bob Marley and the smell of deep fat frying saturated your senses the moment you opened the door.

Text B

The man turned away from her and got out of the car. She stared straight ahead, into the road and put her foot down hard on the accelerator. The engine choked into life again and the car jerked out of the driveway. As the dust raised by her leaving settled, the man contemplated her coming. She had reappeared out of the city she had crawled from like a particularly nasty infectious disease, interrupting his schedule with her demands. Why him? She had plenty of friends who wanted her, so why him and why now, three months after? It didn't make sense and it preyed on his mind, a dull throb behind his eyes. He sighed in disgust at himself, and opening the door, stepped inside.

The man turned away from her and got out of the car. She stared straight ahead, into the road, feeling its freedom and put her foot down hard on the accelerator. The engine choked into life again and she felt the car jerk out of the driveway and away. As the dust behind her settled, she contemplated her leaving. She had come out of his request. And he had the nerve to pretend not to have done. Why him? She had plenty of friends who wanted her, so why him and why now, three months after? It didn't make sense and it preyed on her mind, a shadow of recollection that would not leave. She shook her head in disgust at herself, and slamming on the pedal, charged down the motorway.

Text C

'Bye then.'

'Yeah.'

'Bye.'

continued

'Yeah.'

'Bye, David.'

'Yeah.'

'Oh, I'll see you then.'

I can't resist walking away still facing him. He's turned around using his foot to grind the cigarette butt into the damp sand under the climbing frame. I can imagine his expression: the concentrated look, the way that his eyebrows furrow and his lips purse as if he were about to reach and kiss me. I imagine him pulling me close to him and holding me tight and kissing me right there in the centre of the children's play park, near to the road, with passing motorists watching and lorry drivers beeping their horns and . . . and . . . if only he'd kiss me. I wouldn't be falling over like this, because I'm walking backwards just so that I can stay looking at him for a few more seconds!

I must have made a noise. He's turned around. Quick. Under the slide. Back against the cold wet metal. Too close to the grass. Hay fever. Asthma. Inhaler. Can't breathe. Fight in pocket for inhaler. Deep breath . . . one, two . . . deep breath. Breathing's becoming easier. Still can't relax. I wish he would just hurry up with this confessing his love lark: perhaps, if he could just kiss me, just once, I'd stop making a fool of myself whenever I'm around him.

POINT OF VIEW

As a writer, two questions to ask are: (1) Who is doing the narrating? and (2) From what angle or viewpoint is the action observed by the narrator(s)?

As far as establishing an interesting voice is concerned, the first-person perspective ('I') has a number of advantages. It is immediate and suggests spontaneity. It has the ring of conviction. The narrator who says 'Hey, I was there' has a natural audience. They also have their own personal language quirks. There is considerable potential with first-person narrative, but there are drawbacks as well. Unfortunately, many students cannot maintain distance from their creation and become too subjective and unreflective. Autobiographical pieces of writing need to be crafted with a clear sense of audience.

The third-person, or **omniscient** (all-seeing) narrator, while perhaps unable to capture the vividness of the first-person perspective, is much more flexible in being able to dip in and out of characters' minds in order to see what they are thinking or feeling. The audience can be given a more rounded view of the action and the motivation behind the behaviours.

In the following short extract from Stephen King's *The Shining*, Jack's fevered, disjointed thoughts show that Hallorann was right to feel horror and apprehension: note the way different 'voices' are heard here.

> [Hallorann] ran up the stairs two at a time and stood at the top of the first floor. The blood led down toward the caretaker's apartment. Horror crept softly into his veins and into his brain as he began to walk toward the short hall. The hedge animals had been bad, but this was worse. In his heart he was already sure of what he was going to find when he got down there.
>
> He was in no hurry to see it.
>
> Jack had been hiding in the elevator when Hallorann came up the stairs. Now he crept up behind the figure in the snow-coated parka, a blood-and gore-streaked phantom with a smile upon its face. The roque mallet was lifted as high as the ugly, ripping pain in his back
>
> (?? *did the bitch stick me can't remember??*)
>
> would allow.
>
> 'Black boy,' he whispered. 'I'll teach you to go sticking your nose in other people's business.'

SHOWING, NOT TELLING

The most interesting and effective pieces of writing, whether story, play script or entertaining piece of journalism, are the ones where the writer *shows* the reader, not *tells* them. This may be done in a number of ways.

First, become much more selective in your choice of vocabulary. For example, 'He walked into the room. He was cross' is not nearly as effective as 'He stamped into the room'. Verbs like 'strode', 'marched', 'skipped', 'stumbled' deliver information quickly and without readers being aware they are being fed information.

Think of how you can convey emotion with reference to a gesture of the hands, a shrug, a cough, a frown, a shake of the head. At the same time, let the dialogue carry emotional weight. The opening of Text C (above) shows very clearly the young girl's infatuation ('Bye then . . . Bye . . . Bye, David') and the boy's indifference. A well-presented row or argument can provide a great deal of information in a convincing and authentic way, without everything having to be explained – make your reader do some of the work!

Choose a semantic field to capture the characteristics you want to convey, or focus on one aspect to describe in detail. An interesting exercise, for example, is to indicate the occupation or personality of your characters simply by describing their hands. What might the hands of a policeman/artist/murderer look like? You are literally trying to get inside their skin!

The following extract from Charles Dickens' *David Copperfield* describes Miss Murdstone's character – her name itself suggesting various possible qualities. Her bullying character is shown through the semantic fields of metal, inflexibility and criminality, and the way her appearance is described.

> It was Miss Murdstone who was arrived, and a gloomy-looking lady she was; dark, like her brother, whom she greatly resembled in face and voice, and with very heavy eyebrows, nearly meeting over her large nose, as if, being disabled by the wrongs of her sex from wearing whiskers, she had carried them to that account. She brought with her two uncompromising hard black boxes, with her initials on the lids in hard brass nails. When she paid the coachman she took her money out of a hard steel purse, and she kept the purse in a very jail of a bag which hung upon her arm by a heavy chain, and shut up like a bite. I had never, at that time, seen such a metallic lady altogether as Miss Murdstone was.

Exercise 3

Put into practice what you have read so far in this chapter by answering the following adaptation of an exam board question:

> Read the following quotation carefully:
>
> 'The novelist gives the reader such details about the streets, stores, weather, politics, and concerns of Cleveland (or wherever the setting is) and such details about the looks, gestures, and experiences of the characters that we cannot help believing that the story is true.'
>
> John Gardner, *The Art of Fiction*, 1984
>
> Next, write a story depicting a place and one or two characters, in such a way that your readers 'cannot help believing that the story is true'. Do not make this a static description; you may, if you wish, depict people and places in terms of events and actions.
>
> Write about 850 words if you are doing this for exam practice and up to 2,000 words for coursework.

There are no suggestions for answer to this exercise.

THE EFFECTIVENESS OF HUMOUR

Appropriate humour can really lift a text. This may be a witty comment, an apt pun or wordplay, exaggeration for effect, the twisting of something familiar for effect, or, as Alison Ross in the Intertext series *The Language of Humour* has noted, laughter at the unexpected or incongruous.

Exercise 4

In this extract from *Bridget Jones's Diary* a very ordinary task, a reply to an invitation, is made funny, when the normal expectations of language in use are broken. Comment on how the humour is created here.

> **10 a.m.** Right. I am going to reply to Mark Darcy's invitation and say quite clearly and firmly that I will be unable to attend. There is no reason why I should go. I am not a close friend or relation, and would have to miss both *Blind Date* and *Casualty*.
>
> Oh God, though. It is one of those mad invitations written in the third person, as if everyone is so posh that to acknowledge directly in person that they were having a party and wondered if you would like to come would be like calling the ladies' powder room the toilet. Seem to remember from childhood am supposed to reply in same oblique style as if I am imaginary person employed by self to reply to invitations from imaginary people employed by friends to issue invitations. What to put?
>
> *Bridget Jones regrets that she will be unable ...*
>
> *Miss Bridget Jones is distraught, that she will be unable ...*
>
> *Devastated does not do justice to the feelings of Miss Bridget Jones ...*
>
> It is with great regret that we must announce that so great was Miss Bridget Jones's distress at not being able to accept the kind invitation of Mr Mark Darcy that she has topped herself and will therefore, more certainly than ever, now, be unable to accept Mr Mark Darcy's kind ...

Suggestions for answer to this exercise may be found at the back of the book on page 87.

WRITING TO ENTERTAIN – OTHER IDEAS

Poetry

Poetry writing has a lot of potential if you are a regular writer of poetry, and a whole set of potential problems if you are not. The first of these problems is length. Poetry is by its nature a condensed form. Both written exams and coursework usually require a stipulated length. One way of avoiding this is to present an anthology of poems on a related subject, but even then this may sidestep the requirements of some boards to show that you can write an *extended* piece of work. (One student produced an epic poem 'Courage under Fire' which told the Jackie Robinson story of the first black baseball player in 1930s America, turning a challenging format to his advantage.)

The second problem is that crafting a poem requires very careful consideration. If you decide to make your poem follow a particular metre and rhyme scheme your choices are restricted. Perhaps even greater pitfalls await the writer of 'Free' poetry forms. A poem still has to have a recognisable rhythm and structure.

Make sure your poetry is accessible to your reader. They must be able to make the causal connections with the semantic fields you have chosen. This point is linked to the final pitfall, which is that poetry writing often requires a lengthy commentary to decode what the writer has attempted to do.

Song Writing

With an increasing number of students doing popular music or music technology courses alongside their English courses, song writing is an obvious possibility. Songwriter, musician and visual artist Phil Bird has the following helpful advice, given in an interview for A Level students.

> **Are there differences between creative writing and song writing?**
>
> Perhaps the biggest difference is that prose and poetry are unsupported: they have to stand on their own; there is no melody to enhance any aspect of the words. Poetry specifically has to support itself with its own internal rhythms. Song words on the other hand are supported by the music.
>
> Song lyrics may need a great deal of support, as in the Beatles' 'She Loves You Yeah Yeah Yeah . . . ' as opposed to 'Candle in the Wind', which stands perfectly well on its own. (Look also at the narrative/ballad and a cappella song.) The purpose of song rhythms and melodies is to enable the lyrics and to set the emotional tone.
>
> **Are there rules that have to be adhered to?**
>
> There are no rules; however, as with poetry, it is better to be concrete and specific, rather than general and abstract. Always avoid clichés (moon and June, etc.). Tom Rush could have written '*I feel like a train that's broken down*', but instead he wrote '*I feel like some old engine that's lost its driving wheel*'. Using

specific images in that way makes his work more rhythmic, emotionally vivid and carries the mood better than a generalisation.

Is there a good length to aim for in a lyric?

There's a big difference between long ballads (such as 'Sir Patrick Spens') and a modern two-minute sound bite. Again, it depends on what sort of song you are working on, folk or blues ballad versus *Top of the Pops*. Traditionally, one of the purposes of songs has been a narrative; a way of expressing events, history, relationships, life issues, myths and legends, as well as personal experiences.

Does it help to have a set rhythm to a song?

It helps, but again, rules are there to be broken. If you set up a rhythm, it makes it interesting to have it broken, especially round the chorus or the bridge. It's always useful to have a 'hook' within a song, a catchy, memorable line as a chorus or a riff, such as the Beatles' 'Let it Be' or Simon and Garfunkel's 'Bridge over Troubled Water'. It's also important to have variation within the melody, verse and chorus.

Writing for Children

Writing for children is a popular choice for many students. Yet here too you need to think carefully about your task; otherwise it will be self-penalising. It certainly isn't a case of choosing simple lexis and simple plot accompanied by bright pictures. Not only will you not use language skills sufficiently at this level for either exam or coursework but you will also alienate your intended audience if they think you are patronising them. They are, after all, much closer to the aural tradition of storytelling than you are and are used to listening to effective rhythms and rhymes.

Somerset children's author Beth Webb says:

> Writing for children is about making 'magic' happen. A children's writer needs to enable a child to discover castles in the air, talking animals and wind-flying dragons, tigers who come to tea and a postman who can fix anything, but whether there is a crocodile under the bed or Mum has left Dad, the reader must always feel that somehow, everything will be all right in the end.

So it can be more of a challenge writing for children, not an easy option. However, if you keep the points already mentioned in mind and follow the checklist below, you should write a successful story.

1. You need to know your target audience well. Be prepared to test your story on this audience and redraft extensively in light of comment from them and also from their classroom teacher (if you have gone to your local primary school) and/or carer.
2. Construct a tight, interesting plot with conflict and a resolution.
3. Think carefully about the rhythms and patterns of your story. This is even more important for children who are being read to than for children who can read for themselves. In particular, think of the **prosodic features** of the dialogue: the emphasis on words, the pace and intonation.
4. The characters must be fully realised, the main protagonist engaging and believable. Animals, for example, must have the characteristics of the breed you have chosen to write about. The context must be both appropriate and reliable.

The text below is the climax to a student's story for 7-year-olds. She noted in her commentary that 'because I liked listening to stories as a child, especially the *Brambly Hedge* books, I decided to use some of Jill Barklem's characters for my own story'. She tested her story on a class of 7-year-olds and found that they enjoyed the fast-moving action created by a number of short **declaratives**; repetition that involves sound (popped, banged and splat); and the dialogue. The children also responded with pleasure to the sensory references, especially the sight, smell and taste of food.

Note that suspense and humour guarantee that a relatively high level of lexis is not off-putting, especially as pictures accompany each fifty-word block of text in the original. Successful children's authors such as Roald Dahl and J.K. Rowling are very creative with their lexis, and children cope with unknown words easily because of the contextual support given by the rest of the story and the pictures.

Exercise 5

Read this extract from *After the Storm*; then write your own children's story.

There are no suggestions for answer to this exercise.

From *After the Storm*

'Look up there!' screeched Lilac.

A chubby mouse in a gold waistcoat too small for him was swinging dangerously from the party banners. Everyone screamed with horror.

'It's my Jasper,' breathed Mrs Holly with an anxious sigh. Jasper was always up to mischief. If he was not hiding from his mother, he was being told off at school and standing in the corner.

The chandeliers shook. Balloons popped. Jasper was much too little to be up so high. Everyone watched frantically. His tail was helping him swing back and forth. He was getting faster and faster. The chandeliers swayed and balloons banged. He was sure to fall and injure himself badly.

The tinkling of the chandeliers got louder and louder. Jasper was swinging out of control. His body was swirling sideways and he was struggling to hold onto the banner with his paws. He lost his grip and fell in slow motion, whilst everyone held their breath in fear. Splat! A soft, creamy, melting, deliciously smelling raspberry pavlova saved him! The mice burst into fits of relieved laughter as Jasper quickly tucked into the cake before his mother grabbed him firmly by the ear.

Entertaining Journalism

This chapter has focused on the short story to illustrate entertainment. However, there are other genres, in particular entertaining journalism, that could come under this umbrella. For the purpose of this book, entertaining articles and the sorts of pieces that feature in the 'personal opinion' columns of a newspaper are covered in Chapter 4.

SUMMARY

So, what makes a successful entertaining text?

- A clear sense of writing for a particular audience
- Tight craftsmanship
- Engaging characterisation
- Deft touches, witty description or the creation of a particular atmosphere
- The willingness to be imaginative and take risks
- An overarching point or message
- An authentic 'voice'

WRITING TO ENTERTAIN – SPOKEN TEXTS

CHAPTER 3

INTRODUCTION

It is easy to think simply 'short story' when you are asked to write for the purpose of entertainment. Yet as you have seen from Chapter 2 you must read a lot of short stories, spend time reflecting on narrative strategies and actually have skills in this genre to be successful. There are also other ways of writing to entertain, however, such as the oral media of TV, radio and live interaction, all of which you will be familiar with.

For example, imagine you have been asked to write 'something entertaining with a club setting' for a new magazine for people aged 18 to 25 who enjoy clubbing. The content and style are your own choice, but you should think of your readers relaxing over a cup of coffee or travelling home on the bus as they read your contribution. How could you approach this? Consider scripting with dialogue from your own experience: lively exchanges between fathers and daughters, best friends, bouncers and under-age hopefuls, show-offs and embarrassed beginners. You can use contemporary idioms and speech patterns and capture the sense of natural talk, while clearly conveying character.

It must be made clear at this stage though that all the examples in this chapter are representations of speech. You must never try to 'script the unscripted'; that is, replicate those everyday non-fluency features of speech that occur in spontaneous conversation. And scripting some tasks is simply not feasible. A radio phone-in is never scripted – unless it is part of a fictional drama or narrative. The next time you listen to a sitcom, notice how carefully it is crafted. The characters are allowed to deliver their punch lines without fear of interruption. The canned laughter is introduced in a way that does not cut across any of the utterances. There are few **fillers**, hesitations or false starts. Those that are there are scripted for a particular effect.

THE DRAMATIC MONOLOGUE

The dramatic monologue is a form where one person is addressing an audience in a confidential way. We, the readers, become privileged to read the narrator's innermost thoughts, or, as in the case of Alan Bennett, perhaps the best-known writer of dramatic monologues with his two *Talking Heads* series, to listen to them and see them on screen as well. It is certainly not 'real' talk as such, with all the spontaneous, random, gossipy features that implies, but a good dramatic monologue should have the *feel* of speech and some of its features.

There may be a single point of view, but this does not mean that speech can't be reported from other characters. We all know people who go 'S/he said . . . and I said . . . and then s/he said . . . '. These speech tags are just the sort of chatty and apparently inconsequential detail you can build on to craft your monologue, especially if you have a good ear for natural talk and the ability to represent it convincingly in writing. In his introduction to *Talking Heads* Alan Bennett advises using 'says' or 'said' rather than verbs like 'exclaimed' or 'retorted' because 'in live narration such terms seem literary and self-conscious'. Don't forget that you are at least trying to create the *illusion* that your reader/hearer is the confidant of the narrator. A good way to test whether you have captured the right speaking voice for your character is to video and/or tape your monologue being read aloud (as a 'talking head') and ask your audience for feedback.

One of the most effective creations is the **naïve narrator**, who is quietly allowed to destroy themselves out of their own mouth, while remaining oblivious to what they are revealing and the effect it has on the readers. This gives you some excellent opportunities for irony.

Exercise 1

Read the following extract from Lesley's monologue 'Her Big Chance', in the first series of Alan Bennett's *Talking Heads*. Lesley is being interviewed for a part in a soft-porn film; a fact she does not realise, although the audience do.

Lesley's speech suggests that she is very keen to impress Simon, but that she is unlikely to do this.

1. What features in Lesley's conversation reveal her naïveté?
2. How does Bennett create humour for the audience out of the situation?

'Her Big Chance'

I said, 'Where you may have seen me, Simon, is in *Tess*. Roman Polanski. I played Chloe.' 'I don't remember her,' he said. 'Is she in the book?' I said, 'Book? This is *Tess*, Simon. Roman Polanski. Chloe was the one on the back of the farm cart wearing a shawl. The shawl was original nineteenth-century embroidery. All hand done. Do you know Roman, Simon?' He said, 'Not personally, no.' I said, 'Physically he's quite small but we had a very good working relationship. Very open.' He said that was good, because Travis in the

> film was very open. I said, 'Travis? That's an interesting name, Simon.' He said, 'Yes. She's an interesting character, she spends most of the film on the deck of a yacht.' I said, 'Yacht? That's interesting, Simon. My brother-in-law has a small power boat berthed at Ipswich.' He said, 'Well! Snap!' I said, 'Yes, Small world!' He said, 'In an ideal world, Lesley, I'd be happy to sit here chatting all day but I have a pretty tight schedule and, although I know it's only 9.30 in the morning, could I see you in your bra and panties?'
>
> Extract from *Talking Heads* by Alan Bennett, reproduced by permission of BBC Worldwide Limited. Copyright © Alan Bennett 1988

Suggestions for Answer

The repetition of the speech tags 'I said'/'he said' and the adjective 'interesting' shows just how limited Lesley's vocabulary and ideas are. She has no idea that Roman Polanski's *Tess* is an adaptation of Thomas Hardy's novel *Tess of the D'Urbervilles*, and reveals this in her heavy-handed correction: 'Book? This is *Tess*, Simon.' She then goes on at unnecessary length about Chloe's shawl and suggests that her relationship with Roman Polanski was much closer ('very open') than an extra on the back of a farm cart could possibly have. She refers to her interviewer (whom she assumes wrongly is the director) repeatedly by his christian name, again implying a relationship that does not exist.

The humour arises from the reader's awareness about just how much Lesley is revealing of her ignorance. Despite her desire to seem confident and sophisticated she achieves the opposite effect. There is a considerable difference between the glamour of a yacht and the ordinariness of a power boat at Ipswich. Bennett is here using **bathos** for comic effect. More subtly, there is a suggestion that there is more to this film than acting ability: why else would she be asked to strip to her bra and panties?

Even in this very short extract there really is the illusion that the audience is in direct contact with the narrator, and the narrator's thoughts have the authentic pattern of spoken utterance and identifiable speech habits.

(For more analysis and examples of narrative methods read chapters 4, 'Narrative', and 5, 'Representing Talk', in *The Language of Literature* by Adrian Beard in this series.)

Exercise 2

The following extract is taken from the start of a student's monologue, *A Significant Moment*. The section of commentary accompanying it is included to show that the flat writing is deliberate, and a vehicle for the comic mishap about to befall the pompous narrator. After reading it, write the opening paragraph of your own dramatic monologue, trying to capture the sense of an authentic 'voice'.

A Significant Moment

I am a landscape architect. I grow Cannington Carol, Imperial Star, Argyanthemum, and Alonsoa. I control weeds, using weed killer. I specialise in lawn maintenance. Most lawns in Britain do not need watering, but during occasional dry spells in summer, especially in areas of light soil, to prevent grass from dying back (thereby weakening the lawn), it is best to give a light water. But you must avoid frequent light watering, as this will encourage shallow rooting. The best method for top quality results is to roll, spike, scarify, brush, weed kill, water and feed the lawn. I am a gardener, just like my Charlie. Charlie . . . .

Now I must not digress. The VAC (Village Agricultural Club) is going to Knebworth House to see Charlie next week. Charlie and I are destined to get on. She is a Cancer and I am a Gemini. They make a perfect match, according to the Lonely Heart Club organiser. All my arranged dates have been complete no-hopers. They all turned out to be *Changing Room* fans. The treason! How anyone could prefer Carol Smillie to my Charlie, I will never know.

Commentary

I aimed for my character to show adoration verging on obsession for someone; here it is Charlie Dimmock, from the gardening programme *Groundforce*. The repetition of 'Charlie' with the possessive 'my' creates the idea that Charlie belongs to him, in his mind. The character's obsession is underlined in the piece by the fact that he uses no contractions: 'I am', not 'I'm', for example. His language is precise and fussy.

There is an intentionally boring, monotonous tone to the writing in the first paragraph, with repeated reference to 'I' ('I am' – 'I grow' – 'I control') and simple declaratives in the first four sentences, which show his egocentric nature. The dramatic monologue format indicates that he is a lonely character forced to speak to an imaginary audience.

To help create a plausible piece I researched gardening on the Internet, in particular the site for Knebworth House and Gardens. I have deliberately created a very 'nerdy' character, someone who reads from textbooks for leisure and uses dated expressions.

There are no suggestions for answer to this exercise.

Remember that audiotaping, or simply reading this to your intended audience, is a good way of testing the script. If it can't be read easily and naturally, then it needs drafting until it can. (You may even find that it is easier to say it first on tape and then to write it down, thus catching the speaking voice.)

SKETCH WRITING

You do not need to be a budding comedian to create a successful script, but you do need experience of listening to comedy and an awareness of occupational and social registers, which many of you will be familiar with from other modules of your language or language and literature course.

Exercise 3

The following are two extracts from comedian Harry Enfield's sketches. Text A features DJs Smashie and Nicey. Text B features Kevin the Teenager in 'Perry Goes to Manchester'. Perry, usually the gawky, naïve hero-worshipper of Kevin, has spent a week in Manchester and has returned transformed.

1. What evidence is there of social and occupational registers being used in texts A and B? (*Hint*: Many occupations have a technical vocabulary, or jargon, of their own, with specialised words and phrases. These become a useful shorthand for fellow workers but can exclude outsiders. Similarly, the way a social group speaks marks it as different from other groups. Age, occupation and region will all have an effect on the language used.)
2. What effect do these registers have on their audience?

Text A

SMASHIE: Fab-four-tastic! That was the err, Beatles, err – I love the Beatles, don't you? – with 'Eight Days A Week'.
NICEY: There's only seven days in a week, mate.
SMASHIE: Right, thanks, mate.
NICEY: Don't mention it.
SMASHIE: Erm, but I think you'll find that's what the Beatles – I love the Beatles, don't you? – were saying –
NICEY: I don't care what the Beatles – I love the Beatles, don't you? – were saying, mate, there's only seven days in a week, never longer, never shorter. It's the law!

Text B: Perry Goes to Manchester

[KEV *stares vacantly until the doorbell rouses him. He answers the door.* PERRY *brushes past him walking in an Oasis-style way.*]

PERRY: [*Mancunian accent*] Alright, our Kev?

continued

[KEV *looks vaguely bemused.*]

KEV: Alright, Pel? How was Manchester?
PERRY: Result, sorted, top, mad for it.

[*He takes a defiant swig of Tizer.*]

KEV: Did you go to the Oasis gig?
PERRY: Might have done. Who's asking?
KEV: Well . . . me.
PERRY: Oh right, yeah, sorted, our Kev.
KEV: Were they brilliant?
PERRY: Yeah, sorted, you know, mad for it. I can't remember, I was so out of it.

[*Does a bit of air-punching.*]

Extracts from *Harry Enfield and his Humorous Chums*, reproduced by permission of Penguin Books Limited. Copyright © Harry Enfield 1997

Suggestions for Answer

On initial appearance there is no apparent jargon in the DJs' very short exchange. It could almost be any two men 'talking rubbish' (which is what Harry Enfield himself said they did). This is of course one of the points this sketch is making: neither DJ has much technical expertise. Smashie does, however, try to copy the inventiveness and vitality of contemporary DJs but his expressions are dated. His word coinage – 'Fab-four-tastic!' – is clumsy and the references to the Beatles sets him in a seventies time warp. Smashie is also uncharacteristically hesitant for a DJ, with frequent fillers – 'err' – and breaks in the utterance to include 'I love the Beatles, don't you?' This sentimental utterance becomes a catchphrase used by Nicey as well.

Regional talk and youth **sociolect** form the focus of Kevin's and Perry's sketch. Kevin is in awe of Perry's Mancunian accent and expressions: 'our Kev'. Perry is also using the deliberately elliptical language associated with his age and, perhaps, his gender. However, far from confining himself to one minimal response, he repeats himself again . . . and again: 'Result, sorted, top, mad for it.'

The effect is to poke fun at two recognisable types. The triteness of two DJs, debating the accuracy of 'Eight Days a Week', exposes the fact that they have no expert knowledge and just love the sound of their own voices. Kevin and Perry are desperate to fit in with the prevailing youth culture, which also distances them from other social groups, like those of their parents. (It is no surprise that Kevin's Mum says crushingly later in the sketch: 'Why are you and Perry pretending to be Northerners? You sound very silly.')

Do note at this point how normal non-fluency features may add to the overall effect. Fillers, contractions, hesitations, false starts, repetition, carefully staged interruptions and incomplete utterances give the illusion of real people speaking. Once again, you must remember that even though your own script will have been carefully planned, it must still sound spontaneous.

Exercise 4

You have now explored some of the features that make a successful sketch:

- Narrative structure
- Non-fluency features
- Distinctive speech patterns
- Social/occupational register

Put your ideas into practice by writing the script for the following question, which was set by one of the exam boards:

> A radio comedy programme is looking for new material for a series of sketches that create comedy based on recognisable social and occupational groups. Examples of characters might be game show host, teacher, disc jockey, but you may choose any type of person that would be familiar to the audience.
>
> Write the script for one character as either a monologue or a dialogue. You should capture the distinctive speech habits of the character you choose and exaggerate these to comic effect. Write a script of 700 to 800 words. (If you are doing this task for coursework you may like to write more.)

There are no suggestions for answer to this exercise.

RADIO, TELEVISION, PLAY AND FILM SCRIPTS

What makes a good radio or television play? The answer is that the same features which make any play successful apply to these forms as well. You need to incorporate an initial conflict, then build up dramatic tension and interest by writing effective dialogue and finish with a clear resolution.

Radio Scripts

Radio drama has its own set of unique pros and cons, because of course the audience cannot see the action. This has the immediate advantage that you can set your action wherever you want to and when you want to (for example, in Roman Britain or on the planet Mars), without having to worry about scenery, costume, lighting and so on. Even more significant is the fact that you are not tied by the limitations of a stage – people can go anywhere, do anything. Radio thus offers many possibilities to challenge the imagination and create a picture in the listener's mind.

On the other hand, though, you must pay careful attention to sound. Simply because there aren't any of the usual visual clues, the sound effects, music and dialogue have to do more than in other dramatic media. Sound effects (often written as FX in a script) create atmosphere and give clues about character. Vague sounds like 'tidying a room', which are not immediately identifiable for what they are, do not have the effect, say, of a sigh of exasperation, so be prepared to add identifiable sounds.

There are clear conventions for a radio script. There are also conventions for layout as well.

- A double line of spacing between the end of one scene and the heading for the next is expected.
- Characters' names should appear in capital letters (except in the dialogue).
- Each speaker's name appears to the left of the lines spoken.
- The location of the action and the sound effects required are signalled by capital letters.
- The directions for the characters' mood notes are in lower-case italics and in square brackets (parentheses).
- 'Fade in' and 'Fade out' are used for both radio and television, in radio for sound, in television to indicate the start or finish of a script.

A typical example might be the following:

OUTDOORS. CLAMOUR OF THE FUNFAIR

ANGUS: Fancy a go on the Big Dipper?
JULIE: [*startled but pleased at the same time*] D'you really mean it? I've been summing up the courage all afternoon, but [*laughing*] I didn't want to go on my own.
ANGUS: [*moving off*] Well, come on then!
JULIE: [*calling after him*] Wait! I'm coming. . . .

(*Fade*)

You need to use these conventions with subtlety. Actor-manager Timothy West wrote a parody of the conventions of radio drama entitled, predictably, *This Gun I Have in my Right Hand is Loaded*. The action starts with a ridiculous series of noises that include traffic, wind, ships' sirens, a dog barking and a hansom cab, followed by echoing footsteps, a rattling key chain, the door opening and then closing. These actions so obviously indicate Husband Returning Home that his wife's 'Who's that?' is totally unnecessary. This is underlined further by his reply, in which he tells her that it is her husband.

Think carefully about differentiating your characters. Four teenage girls from the same class going home by bus to the same housing estate will require considerable ability from the actors performing the script if the listening audience are to distinguish them aurally. Creating a range of characters of different ages, genders and regional accents will help to avoid confusion. Keep your characters consistent as well. Rosemary Horstmann, in the 'Writing Handbooks' series *Writing for Radio*, suggests that a useful exercise is to read aloud all the lines given to one character, end to end in sequence, leaving out the speeches in between. 'This will often throw up lines which are patently out of character, and places where characterisation can be strengthened.' You may also find lines that are neither forwarding the plot, helping to establish character nor creating atmosphere. Remove them: every word must count.

A final note on the radio medium, which applies not only to radio dramas but also to features and documentaries as well. Radio is very intimate. It may be broadcast to millions, but it carries its message to individuals through their ears alone, and individuals, moreover, who may be doing something else at the time, or have switched on late and missed the opening introduction. Keep your audience in mind all the time. Don't forget that listeners have to accept broadcast information in the order in which it is presented; they can't reread a passage. So structure your text clearly and continue to give helpful contextual information. Avoid 'white silence'; that is, when absolutely nothing can be heard. Keeping your audience in suspense when they can see you is one thing, but you must script any 'meaningful pauses' on radio carefully. In addition, think about your audience's sensibilities. Many radio listeners are offended by swearing and taboo talk. It is a test of your linguistic ability to create scenes which may suggest social realism without using any offensive language at all.

Exercise 5

Look at a copy of the *Radio Times* and note when radio drama is being scheduled. Every day of the week the BBC broadcasts a play on at least one of its domestic services, in particular Radio 4, with its 'Afternoon Play'. Before attempting your own radio play, familiarise yourself with a range of different styles and authors' work.

There are no suggestions for answer to this exercise.

Television and Film Scripts

The conventions for writing for television also need careful consideration. Once you know what a script looks like on the page and have watched a few of your favourite programmes critically, observing how tension is created or humour developed, you can write your own script.

Here are some of the conventions for writing a television script:

- Scenes are always numbered consecutively
- INT or EXT is used to denote interior or exterior setting
- Where the scene takes place (e.g. WILSON'S KITCHEN) is always stipulated in the heading
- DAY or NIGHT: an indication of when the scene takes place is always necessary
- VO (Voice over) is used for narration
- OOV is sometimes used as shorthand for Out of Vision. The character can be heard but not seen
- POV (Point of view) is used when you would like something to be seen from a particular character's standpoint (e.g. FROM RON WILSON'S POV)
- Etiquette suggests that you do not stipulate too many specific camera angles: that is the director's job. You may want to suggest a specific CLOSE-UP, MEDIUM SHOT or LONG SHOT. Apart from this, the only other terms you might use are PAN, where the camera moves slowly in a horizontal sweep (though this is more usual in a film script) and CUT TO, which is an abrupt shift from one camera angle to another

Exercise 6

Read the following extract from the BAFTA-winning comedy *The Office*. David Brent is a petty, pompous boss who thinks he's the funniest, most popular man in the world. In this scene, taken from the first episode in Series 1, he is showing the new temp, Ricky, around.

What do we learn about:

1. Brent
2. Gareth
3. Tim?

Explore the ways they have been characterised in this episode.

Suggestions for answer to this exercise may be found at the back of the book on page 87.

SCENE 16. INT DESK AREA. DAY

SHOTS OF PEOPLE WORKING, THEN CUT TO: BRENT LEADING RICKY THROUGH THE OFFICE. HE GRINS EXCITEDLY AND PAUSES TO POINT OUT A 'FLAT ERIC' DOLL IMPALED ON A COAT STAND. HE WAITS FOR A BIG LAUGH. HE RECEIVES A BEMUSED SILENCE. UNFAZED, HE POINTS TO TIM.

BRENT: You've met Tim, haven't you?
RICKY: Hello.
TIM: Hello, alright?

[BRENT SCOOTS OVER TO GARETH.]

BRENT: Ooh, careful, watch this one! Gareth Keenan in the area!

[MAKING THE INTRODUCTIONS]

Ricky, the new temp.
GARETH: Alright?
RICKY: Good to see you.
BRENT: Introduce yourself.
GARETH: Erm . . . Gareth Keenan, Assistant Regional Manager.
BRENT: Assistant to the Regional Manager.

[BRENT POINTS TO HIMSELF.]

BRENT: Gareth's my right-hand man, immediately beneath me . . . ooh, as an actress said to a bishop! No, he's not. I'm not. . . .

[TIM LOOKS ON.]

BRENT: Tell 'em about your car and your kung fu and everything.
GARETH: Er . . . yeah, I've got a TR3. I bought it for twelve hundred, done it up, now it's worth three grand.
BRENT: Profit on that.
GARETH: Suspension, new engine. . . .
BRENT: It was just a wreck . . .
GARETH: Respray . . .
BRENT: . . . Built it himself . . .
GARETH: I've got some photos.

[HE OPENS HIS DRAWER TO GET THE PHOTOS, BUT RECOILS IN HORROR.]

GARETH: Oh, what is that?
BRENT: Woh, woh, woh, woh.

[GARETH POINTS AT TIM.]

GARETH: Right, that is it.
BRENT: Slow down, you move too fast. Solomon's here. All part of the job. What's going on?
GARETH: He's put my stapler inside a jelly again.

[GARETH HOLDS UP A JELLY, WHICH WAS HIDDEN IN HIS DRAWER. TIM TRIES TO LOOK INNOCENT.]

Extract from *The Office: The Scripts, Series 1* by Ricky Gervais and Steve Merchant. Reproduced by permission of PFD

The conventions for writing screenplays are slightly different. Whereas radio plays are highly verbal, film screenplays are highly visual. The layout includes lower case for the description of the action taking place and you may find you want to refer to more different types of shot and camera angle. Published screenplays are widely available, so you can study layouts yourself. The following is the opening of a student's film script:

Doomed Youth

Opening title sequence

Black screen, titles, melancholy piano music gradually fades into noise of the first scene. . . .

EXT FRANCE BATTLEFIELD DAY

The scene is chaos. It is the middle of a barrage. There is an unbearable amount of noise. Pan across no-man's land. It is the afternoon darkness of mid-winter, the scene is shrouded in a gloom which is intermittently broken by the explosions of flares overhead, illuminating the scene in an eerie glow.

Shells are exploding, creating huge craters. Blood drains into the mud of no-man's land, finding its way into shell holes and turning the stagnant water scarlet. Dead and wounded lie where they fell, among the stumps of decimated trees and shell-churned earth.

The camera zooms in on a boot protruding from the side of the parapet and a rat scurrying beneath it. Pan over into a British trench. The barbed wire protecting the line vibrates violently, as if it were desperately trying to escape the scene. The duckboard rattles and shakes.

The camera tracks downwards on to WILLIAM, cowed in a sentry post. He rocks backwards and forwards, his head between his knees. He is repeating something over and over to himself; it is inaudible over the noise of the barrage, but grows louder as he lifts his head.

WILLIAM: Bastards. Bastards.

Notice how the camera does a series of establishing shots before moving in to focus on William. By filming him from above his vulnerability is accentuated. There is also very little speech here compared to a typical piece of radio drama.

AND NOW FOR SOME IDEAS FOR PLOTS

To finish this chapter here are a few ideas to help you, whether you favour radio, television or film as your medium.

1. The journey of discovery. Your character may literally take a journey. It is often the case that we don't find out what a person is like until they are taken out of their usual environment. On the other hand, the discovery may be an internal one, a journey of self-awareness.
2. The triumph over adversity. This is a common theme in the soaps on our screen, but watch that you don't over sentimentalise. We all like to see the disadvantaged and those with a handicap of some sort 'win through'.
3. The well-established circle of friends is destroyed by the (glamorous/dangerous) outsider. This is a tried and true formula in *Hollyoaks*, *Neighbours*, *Buffy the Vampire Slayer* and so on.

Spoken forms are discussed further in Chapter 4, where the news editor for a radio station gives his advice for writing informatively for radio, and in the first half of Chapter 6, which explores spoken forms for a persuasive purpose: speech writing and multimedia advertising.

SUMMARY

In this chapter you have explored:

- The conventions of a number of spoken forms
- The differences between radio, television and drama forms
- The ways naturalistic dialogue may be achieved
- Examples of social and occupational registers
- Narrative and plot structure
- Writing and the different genres chosen

WRITING TO INFORM CHAPTER 4

INTRODUCTION

Writing to inform often encourages interesting and imaginative writing. At one end of the scale this writing could easily find itself in the 'entertainment' category instead. You have been reminded throughout this book that many texts have more than one purpose. The important thing to remember if you have to provide a folder that contains texts with different purposes is to make sure that the *primary* purpose of each, whether entertainment, information, instruction or persuasion, is different.

THE PERSONAL VOICE

The Feature Article

Entertaining journalism, such as a non-fiction narrative, is often referred to by editors as a 'feature' article, and is achieved by writing about a topic from a personal viewpoint and a particular angle. This must involve real knowledge/research, however. Articles on topics such as learning to drive, passing exams, relationship problems and peer group pressure (in other words, areas in which you may well have vivid and interesting first-hand experience), can be particularly successful.

You have the opportunity to produce 'real' writing; writing that can be and does get published. Newspapers and magazines often invite opinion in the form of competition articles. Contributions to community/college booklets and magazines are topical and again have the ring of authenticity that comes from being aimed at a real audience. Some pieces can even have unexpected benefits: the student who was fed up with the continual lateness of his bus to college organised a questionnaire among fellow students using the same bus, turned his findings into an article for his local newspaper, and sent both article and survey to the bus company concerned. The student got a more punctual bus service and a good piece of coursework!

The secret to writing good entertaining journalism is to have something to say which you know about; in other words, follow your own interests and talents.

Exercise 1

Read the following article, which won a local newspaper competition for a 500-word article seeking an individual view 'through the eyes of a student'. Besides providing the theme, the *Taunton Times* stipulated that the piece had to be 'lively and personal'.

Make notes on the following:

1. Comment on the length of the article.
2. Analyse the discourse structure – the way the arguments are organised.
3. What is the main sentence type used here?
4. What rhetorical and literary devices are used to maintain reader interest?

Through the Binoculars of a Student Birder

If asked my opinion of Taunton's nightlife, my response would probably describe which owls I had seen or heard in the area recently. I am a teenage birder and I am far more interested in the nearby nightlife in terms of nature than the clubbing kind of nightlife. My ideal stress-release is to visit my 'local patch' in the outskirts of Taunton, Somerset, and spend hours searching for and watching our feathered-friends. I have a far greater knowledge of the birds at my local patch than the ones down at my local pub.

Not many people realise what a diversity of wildlife can be found so close to home, and I came across my own wealth of wildlife by complete accident. Whilst strolling along a stream I came across a field of cows and one hugely muscular bull. I ventured intrepidly along the path, getting as close to the hedge as physically possible, but on my return I found the herd was determined to make things inconvenient, and had blocked my only safe passage. I decided not to get between the bull and his female companions so I took a route home along some rural lanes. The detour killed two birds with one stone really; I got home safely and found an abundance of bird life, and so I have been returning as often as I can.

I get strange looks all the time (only when I'm birding I mean – or at least I hope it's only then), simply because people don't see the stereotypical teenager as a birdwatcher. I once found myself being chased by three dogs which had been sent by a misunderstanding farmer. I had my bike and so at least I had the chance of escape but they were accomplished at this sport and to my terror they could even master cattle grids. Thankfully I lived to bird another day.

Though birding provides an escape from my worries, the area itself isn't worry free. You may consider it a pessimistic view, but in reality, my favourite spot is under threat from destruction. As plans to provide more housing in Taunton

> are continually proposed, the outskirts steadily become developed. In my own wildlife haven the rural paths could become pavements, the trees lampposts and the cows cars. In the future, clubbing birds may replace my wild nocturnal birds. Regrettably, Keats' famous line, 'Thou wast not born for death, immortal bird!' does not speak the truth of today's bird life, and nowadays larks are descending faster than they are ascending.
>
> Although there is a threat from the field-eating monster of urbanisation, my local patch is for now, still tranquil, in its own way. The countryside is subtly resisting development; historic looking tractors block the whole width of lanes, dogs growl as you wander past them (some houses noticeably let their dogs out when you approach), and the amiable-looking cows are quietly making devious plans to keep you away. I just hope that it remains this way.

Suggestions for Answer

The length

You probably noticed how short this piece is. Feature articles need to be short and punchy to suit the layout requirements of a newspaper or magazine, usually about 1,000 words. In the competition above, the 500-word requirement was imposed as a discipline to make students think about their writing very carefully. The 500-word limit means that the piece has to be tightly controlled. Every word has to be effective in its positioning and meaning. 'The field-eating monster of urbanisation', for example, concisely sums up the writer's dismay that his wildlife habitats are being taken over by the need for land to put houses on, as well as his rage about this fact, captured in the emotive 'monster'.

The discourse structure

The first three paragraphs are a light-hearted play on the words 'nightlife' and 'bird'. The fourth paragraph has a more serious point as the focus switches from a personal to a universal theme: progress brings destruction. The final paragraph returns to the present and to the writer's own personal response to the threat to his beloved wildlife.

The sentence structure

There are a number of short declaratives that suit the requirements of the word length and the tone of the piece. The style is quite condensed. Note the contrastive pairs in a list of three: 'Rural paths could become pavements, the trees lampposts and the cows cars.'

Rhetorical and literary devices

The personification of the 'devious' cows and the 'subtly resisting' countryside makes a witty but still implicitly serious point. The inclusion of the line by Keats adds sophistication, hinting at the rural paradise associated with the Romantic period when he was writing. A second recognisable intertextual phrase (the skylark reference) is also added for humorous purposes.

Exercise 2

Now write your own article 'through the eyes of a student' on *either* the joys/perils of part-time work, *or* being a teenager in the twenty-first century ('They Just Don't Understand Us!'), *or* peer group pressure. Do not exceed 1,000 words. Aim this *either* as an amusing article for your local newspaper *or*, in the case of the first option, as part of an employer's/organisation's training manual.

There are no suggestions for answer to this exercise.

Know Your Genre

Knowing the conventions of your genre will help you to write with confidence and appropriateness.

Newspapers

If you are writing for an exam, you will not, of course, be able to replicate a number of the graphological features associated with a newspaper, but it is quite sufficient to indicate in the margin or the commentary that these features would be used in the published version. Some of the more specialised features are difficult to reproduce in coursework as well, so again you can indicate where these would be. Don't forget that you are being assessed on your writing skills and your awareness of the **graphology** associated with a particular genre.

When writing an article for a newspaper, keep the following discourse features in mind:

- The *headline* is in banner form and may have a number of functions. The best headlines are snappy, eye-catching and encapsulate the meaning (the following headlines are all from the *Sun*). They may use alliteration: 'What a Difference a Di makes' (one of many 'Di' references when Princess Diana was alive); assonance: 'Who Told That Chopper Whopper?' during the Westland helicopter row; puns: 'L'Ambush' on a story about the French hijacking of British lamb lorries during the 1980s; or intertextuality: when lowly Caledonian Thistle beat mighty Celtic, the *Sun* headline read: 'Super Caly Go Ballistic, Celtic Are Atrocious.'
- The *subheading* is an additional heading under the main heading.
- The *standfirst* is an introductory paragraph often emboldened and separated from the main article.

- The *byline* is an important feature in establishing a journalistic feel to your piece. At its simplest you simply declare your authorship: 'By Joe Bloggs', for example. You can integrate the byline by writing 'Joe Bloggs asks/writes/wonders/explores' and so on.
- A telling picture with a suitable *caption* underneath will hook the reader.
- The text is written in *columns* – only worth replicating in coursework.
- Features that may be difficult to replicate in your own writing are the *drop letter*, in which the first letter of the article extends over two to three lines, and the *pull-quote*, where a snappy quotation is 'pulled' out of the text. (See the article 'Hard Times For Magwitch's Marsh' in Chapter 1.)

Stylistic features

Start with a 'hook' to get your reader interested. Whether this is a dramatic headline or an interesting anecdote or a personalised account (or all three), you need something to keep your reader's attention. Scour the newspapers and the Net for interesting titbits. You can 'revisit' worn-out themes with a topical reference. Lifestyle choices can be introduced with anecdotes about celebrities in the limelight, for example.

Use modifiers. These can be emotive ('*sensational* victory', '*evil* dictator', '*proud* parents'), or provide information ('*17-year-old* Wayne Rooney, *youngest England player yet*'). Although a broadsheet will often use longer and more complex sentences than a tabloid, both employ a condensed style and are mindful of word limits. 'Eyewitness James Brown, a neighbour of the deceased' would always be preferred to 'James Brown, who witnessed the attack and is a neighbour of the deceased...'. The subordinate clause, introduced by the relative pronoun 'who', seems too wordy here.

The Plain English Society's advice is that short sentences are best for conveying factual information to a general audience. Fifteen to twenty words are suggested for most sentences.

Journalese is the term used to describe words that come to be associated with newspapers, such as particularly dramatic, forceful verbs 'crack down', 'storm', 'slam' (often a plan or decision, not a door!). Collocation, or a group of words often found together, is another feature used by journalists, mainly in the tabloids ('sex symbol', 'love rat'). The liveliness of the writing is often reinforced with alliteration and puns. Careful use of colloquial language, slang, idioms, memorable inventive phrasing and vocabulary will lift your writing.

Your approach may be personal or provocative, but should not be so extreme as to irritate a wide audience. Try to establish a sense of shared experience and adopt the appropriate level of formality for your readership. Capturing an effective relationship between the voice in the text and the narratee, the implied reader of your text, is a key discriminator in the overall effectiveness of your work.

Your paragraphs should signal a thread of argument, as well as a sequence of points and evidence. There should be an effective variety of sentence structures, which may include **minor sentences**, for effect. Your ending should be a satisfactory, lively conclusion. You can round off your article with details for your reader to get further information if necessary, such as names and contact addresses, including email addresses and telephone numbers.

Exercise 3

The following are the openings to three feature articles on British 'national institutions' – of different sorts! Choose one of the titles, or invent one of your own for another 'national institution'. Decide which type of newspaper you are going to write for. Name the newspaper and choose an article from the paper as a style model. Make sure that you are familiar with the style of that paper.

Then research and write your own informative article (750 to 1,000 words).

> **Text A: Radcliffe's Brave Feats Leave Her Walking on Air**
>
> One year ago Paula Radcliffe broke the bars of her cage; yesterday she took wing.
>
> [This was written after Paula beat her own world record in the London Marathon.]
>
> Extract from *The Times*, 14 April 2003. Reproduced by permission of News International Syndication

> **Text B: Creeper Control**
>
> It brightens up winter and feeds the birds. Don't knock ivy, tame it.
>
> Originally from a weekend gardening column

> **Text C: The Nightmare That Is Valentine's Day**
>
> It's fake, forced and rarely fun. Worse, it's the day of triumph for the Creepy Couple.
>
> Originally from the *Sunday Times Style* magazine, 9 February 2003

Magazine writing

The features mentioned above apply largely to writing for a magazine, although in a double-page spread, for example, you have more flexibility of layout and you may choose to use a strapline (an additional headline above the main headline) and an endsign, which is a dot or square that signifies the end of the article (so that your reader doesn't have to turn the page).

In addition, consider using fact boxes (e.g. 'Top Tips', 'Ten Points to Remember'), question-and-answer formats, bullets, subheadings and more varied type sizes and fonts. Eye-catching pictures, cartoons or graphics will draw your reader in, as will using colour. Finally, arrange separate blocks of text on your page so that they don't look dense and off-putting. This is called 'white space'. (If you are sitting an exam, you can achieve the same effect by leaving a line or two of space.)

For further information on text types, especially word-processing packages that enable you to check a piece of text for levels of formality and style, read Chapter 6 of Shaun O'Toole's *Transforming Texts* in this series.

Writing information for radio

Mike James, News Editor of Minster FM, has the following tips for those interested in the conventions of writing for radio news programmes.

> A radio script must be written as you speak. There are a few simple rules. Use abbreviations ('they are' becomes 'they're'), use short sentences (these are easier to read), and read the script back to yourself. A strange phenomenon in a radio newsroom is everyone talking to their computers!
>
> Generally a script for a news bulletin should be no longer than three or four sentences (this applies to everything from commercial stations to Radio 4). This may not seem much, especially compared to newspaper articles, but any longer and you start to lose your audience. In the same way, if you are writing a longer packaged piece there should be no more than three or four sentences in between each piece of audio.
>
> As well, write as if the story is ongoing, even if it's in the past tense. Things 'have been happening', rather than something 'happened'. Avoid phrases you wouldn't normally use; always write in the simplest terms without dumbing down. It's a case of making it sound natural.

Reviews

Writing music or film reviews for a selected magazine is a popular choice among students. Magazines such as *Kerrang!*, *NME*, *Raw* and *Q* provide effective models, since they have a recognisable style and comment on music and musicians with which students are often highly familiar. However, do treat music reviews in general with caution. Some articles resort to offensive language or crude stereotypes in order to be noticed in a crowded market. As always, think about your purpose as well as your audience. Are you communicating your opinion clearly and accessibly? Are you informing your reader about a period, style, technique or example of popular culture? Will your text also serve that other purpose of being assessed for an exam?

Exercise 4

Before you attempt writing a music review, read the review for a performance of 'The Star Spangles', printed in *Kerrang!*. What are its most obvious features?

THE STAR SPANGLES
02.04.03
The 100 Club, London
KKKK
A stellar spectacle in the capital.

THE STAR Spangles execute their rock 'n' roll in a way that's so damn tight, you'd never suspect their frontman of having the loosest lips in rock. Not that Ian Wilson is much of a talker; tonight his rapport with the crowd is built more on the evil choirboy scowls and mad-eyed stares he shoots in our direction. But it's his unwieldy lips, which stretch and contort into all manner of impossible shapes, that tell us all we need to know about The Star Spangles. For although the New York quartet are handsome enough to elicit comparisons with The Strokes, these are no cookie cutter garage-rockers.

From Wilson's scraggy, post-'Scissorhands' barnet to his sandpaper vocals, The Star Spangles are carving a niche as evil anti-hipsters sent to haunt the hollow carcass of nu-garage rock with their ghoulish bubblegum punk.

Even before they launch into an explosive rendition of 'Which Of The Two Of Us Is Gonna Burn This House Down?' the Spangles clearly thrive on shaking up the prescribed punk rock aesthetic. Decked out in a gray, four-button suit, pink shirt and slightly jazzy tie, his oil spill hair sticking out in tufts, Wilson looks almost Sunday-School respectable. Until, that is, he starts indulging in a nervous tic which involves yanking invisible lice out of his hair and throwing them on the floor. It's this apparent fascination with the sick and infected underside of life that makes The Star Spangles a more inspired phenomenon than their garage-punk peers. Whether they're setting a pseudo-Victorian myth to a vehement guitar volley on 'The Sins Of A Family Fall On The Daughter' or stating their case as fame-hating loners on 'Stay Away From Me', The Star Spangles are turning populist garage-punk on its head. They might be a magnet for fashionistas, but Wilson has a comic quality that raises them above preconceived notions of 'cool'. When a beer glass is hurled in the direction of the stage, he flinches and raises an eyebrow in exaggerated fashion, endearing himself to the crowd in an instant.

Combining the dazzle of a shooting star with the darkness of a winter's night, The Star Spangles are truly a sight (and sound) to behold.

JANE GILLOW

Figure 4.1 'The Star Spangles' by Jane Gillow

Extract from a review in *Kerrang!*, 12 April 2003, reproduced by permission of Emap Performance

Suggestions for Answer

Note the mix of high-order lexis with Latinate terms ('elicit', 'pseudo'), and references to field-specific terms in the music industry, as well as colloquial expression and near taboo forms. There is lexical flexibility. 'Fashionistas' is a **coinage**, and there are a number of compounds such as 'cookie-cutter'. The semantic field of stars is combined with the semantic fields of illness and evil. The melodrama is piled on with the **hyperbole** ('his unwieldy lips, which stretch and contort into all manner of . . . shapes'), and there are a number of contrasts: ('tight rock 'n' roll'/'loosest lips'). As in many similar reviews, there is also considerable creativity in the phonology, with frequent alliteration, dynamic verbs whose sound reflects the sense, 'launch', 'yanking', 'hurled', and **assonance** ('bubblegum punk').

The flippant humour, exaggeration for effect and the level of metaphorical and lexical inventiveness, which have become a trademark of such reviews, are not easy to replicate effectively. Be warned!

The interview

The branch of investigative journalism where you interview someone who has something interesting to say can provide an excellent informative piece. However, you need to prepare for this carefully if it is to be convincing. Here is the opening to an interview, printed in *Q*.

> **MADONNA Attacks!**
>
> Madonna arrives on time, looking as inconspicuous as the most famous woman in the world can. She is dressed down in chocolate brown and charcoal, with a tweed cap pulled down low over her eyes.
>
> 'Hi, I'm Madonna,' she says, as she squeezes, with some inelegance, into our corner booth. Heads do not turn as readily as they might, thanks to her newly brunette hair.

In the above interview care is taken not only to establish Madonna's appearance and status, but also the effect she has on the interviewer and bystanders. In addition, her actual speech is quoted to capture a sense of 'real' talk.

It is impossible to write with such confidence about a purely imaginary interview. What is more, can you convince your reader that this is an informative article rather than an entertaining piece? One exam board has actually said that an interview with a celebrity (real or imagined) cannot be invented. Don't forget the opening of this book: 'Some of the best writing breaks the rules'! However, it takes skill and you need to prepare your groundwork thoroughly. Turn your imagined interview into a satirical piece, exaggerating the known features of your celebrity, and it could work. For example, a student, mindful of the recent publicity about the stress levels of football managers, 'interviewed' one in a health food café. The manager's preoccupation with the advisability of drinking a cup of coffee and allowing himself a slice of carrot cake after his modest salad really lifted the piece and gave it humour.

However, you do not need to go to famous people for interesting interviews. Older members of the family, friends or local 'characters' will have interesting experiences to recount. Prepare a list of possible questions but be prepared to be flexible and follow up promising diversions. If your interviewee doesn't mind, record your interview. (Always get permission first.) Then you can integrate some authentic quotations when you write it up.

Exercise 5

Now answer the following question, adapted from an exam board question:

> Following a successful series on people's lives at the turn of the twentieth century, the editor of a local paper intends to run a new series of articles on people's lives at the start of the twenty-first century. Each article will focus on the life of someone over the age of 30. You have been asked to write two of these articles. Write about two people you know well.
>
> Concentrate on vivid detail rather than a mini-biography, ensuring that your writing is genuinely informative about attitudes and experiences today. The articles should interest the readers of newspapers and also the social historian of the future. The editor requires you to write in the third person. Each article should be about 500 words.

There are no suggestions for answer to this exercise.

THE PUBLIC VOICE – INVESTIGATION AND PUBLIC INFORMATION

Who 'Owns' the Text?

The examples you have looked at so far in this chapter freely express personal experience or personal opinion. If you are writing on behalf of an organisation you have to be very careful to avoid such an obviously personal voice.

For example, take a task popular with students. This is writing an information pack to be sent to a community in, say, the USA, with which your own local community has arranged an exchange. You have been asked to write that part of the pack dealing with the features and way of life of your local community, including possible day trips within the vicinity. You may feel this gives you a golden opportunity to extol the virtues (or the lack of) in your community, with very little apparent effort. After all, you will be well aware of the entertainment possibilities for your own age group. However, if it is aimed solely (or even mainly) at your own age group and their interests, it hasn't succeeded. You must take into account whole families and their requirements. You need to investigate facilities and entertainment for the very young and the older age group or those with special needs.

In addition, you are writing on behalf of the community. Keep your tone inviting but not overly enthusiastic (you are informing, not persuading) and avoid cynicism. At the same time, ensure that your text is both worthwhile and lively, with a mixture of practical information and background interest, and that it includes variations in the presentation of the text and accompanying illustration.

The Issue of Formality

The level of formality you are going to use will be vital to success in this sort of writing. (For further analysis of ideas about formality see the book *How Texts Work* by Adrian Beard in this series.)

Exercise 5

Read the following extracts from two information publications on drugs. Text A is 'Drugs and Solvents: A Young Person's Guide' (Figure 4.2). Text B is 'The Score: Facts About Drugs' (Figure 4.3). Both were produced by the Health Education Authority.

Answer the following questions:

1. What features are used to make the material as clear as possible?
2. What point of view is used?
3. What graphological features are used to attract the reader? (Note that both the originals were in colour. Text A had green dots on a yellow background for the numbering, and the title was orange. Text B had white writing on a bold red and black background on one side, and a swirl of colours on the other.)
4. What indications are there that these extracts were written for different age groups?

Suggestions for answer to this exercise may be found at the back of the book on page 88.

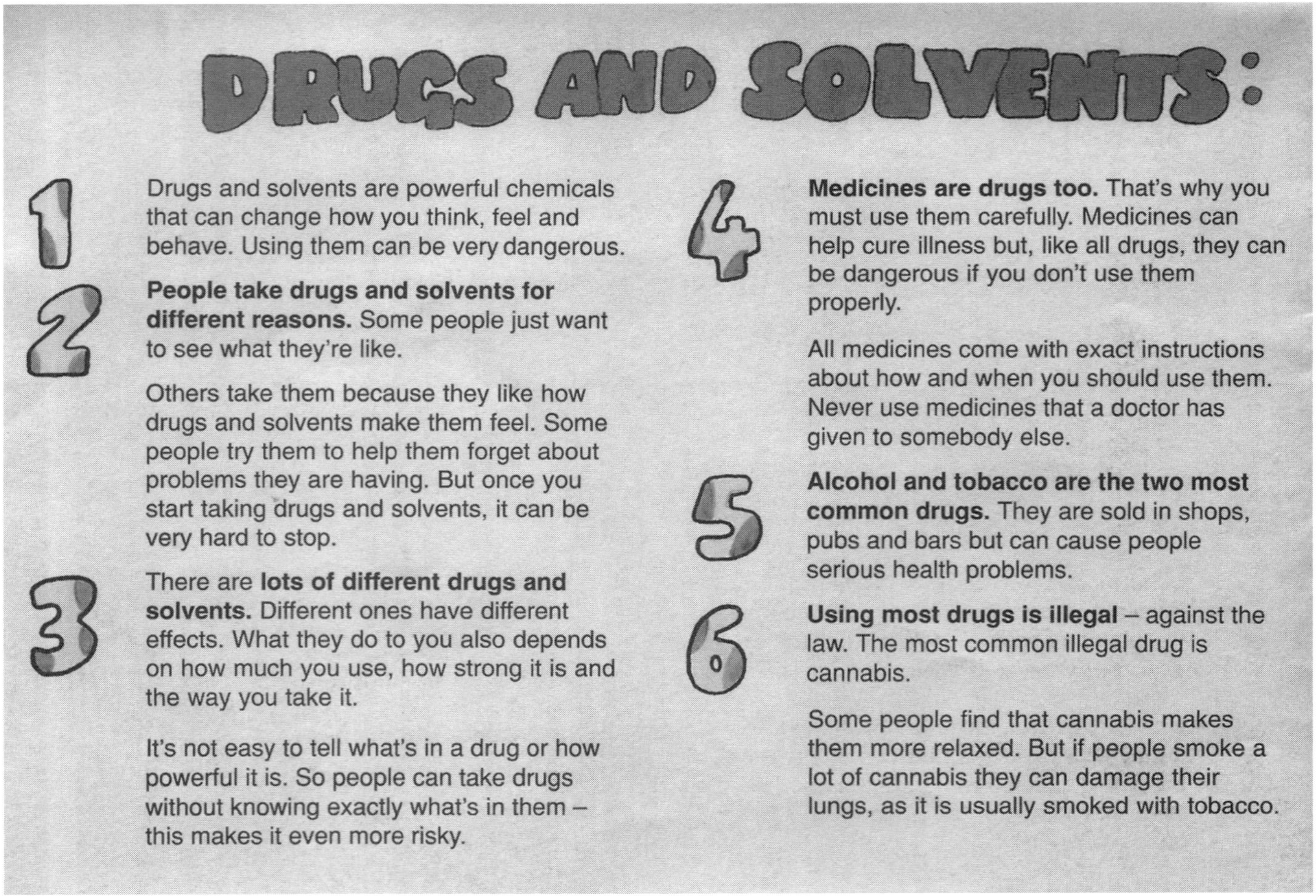

DRUGS AND SOLVENTS:

1 Drugs and solvents are powerful chemicals that can change how you think, feel and behave. Using them can be very dangerous.

2 **People take drugs and solvents for different reasons.** Some people just want to see what they're like.

Others take them because they like how drugs and solvents make them feel. Some people try them to help them forget about problems they are having. But once you start taking drugs and solvents, it can be very hard to stop.

3 There are **lots of different drugs and solvents.** Different ones have different effects. What they do to you also depends on how much you use, how strong it is and the way you take it.

It's not easy to tell what's in a drug or how powerful it is. So people can take drugs without knowing exactly what's in them – this makes it even more risky.

4 **Medicines are drugs too.** That's why you must use them carefully. Medicines can help cure illness but, like all drugs, they can be dangerous if you don't use them properly.

All medicines come with exact instructions about how and when you should use them. Never use medicines that a doctor has given to somebody else.

5 **Alcohol and tobacco are the two most common drugs.** They are sold in shops, pubs and bars but can cause people serious health problems.

6 **Using most drugs is illegal** – against the law. The most common illegal drug is cannabis.

Some people find that cannabis makes them more relaxed. But if people smoke a lot of cannabis they can damage their lungs, as it is usually smoked with tobacco.

Figure 4.2 'Drugs and Solvents: A Young Person's Guide'
Reproduced by permission of Crown Copyright

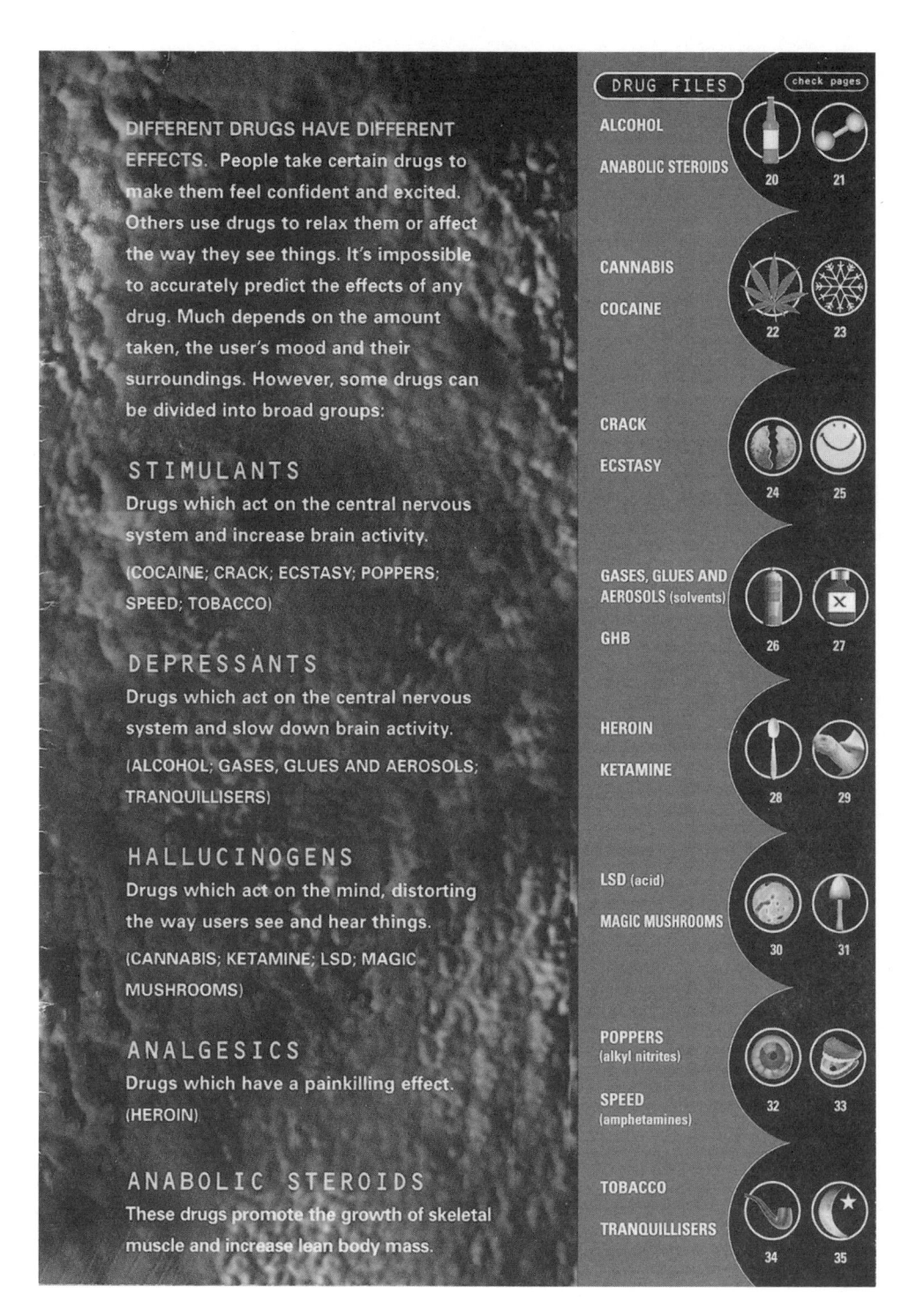

DIFFERENT DRUGS HAVE DIFFERENT EFFECTS. People take certain drugs to make them feel confident and excited. Others use drugs to relax them or affect the way they see things. It's impossible to accurately predict the effects of any drug. Much depends on the amount taken, the user's mood and their surroundings. However, some drugs can be divided into broad groups:

STIMULANTS
Drugs which act on the central nervous system and increase brain activity.
(COCAINE; CRACK; ECSTASY; POPPERS; SPEED; TOBACCO)

DEPRESSANTS
Drugs which act on the central nervous system and slow down brain activity.
(ALCOHOL; GASES, GLUES AND AEROSOLS; TRANQUILLISERS)

HALLUCINOGENS
Drugs which act on the mind, distorting the way users see and hear things.
(CANNABIS; KETAMINE; LSD; MAGIC MUSHROOMS)

ANALGESICS
Drugs which have a painkilling effect.
(HEROIN)

ANABOLIC STEROIDS
These drugs promote the growth of skeletal muscle and increase lean body mass.

DRUG FILES — check pages

Drug	Page
ALCOHOL	20
ANABOLIC STEROIDS	21
CANNABIS	22
COCAINE	23
CRACK	24
ECSTASY	25
GASES, GLUES AND AEROSOLS (solvents)	26
GHB	27
HEROIN	28
KETAMINE	29
LSD (acid)	30
MAGIC MUSHROOMS	31
POPPERS (alkyl nitrites)	32
SPEED (amphetamines)	33
TOBACCO	34
TRANQUILLISERS	35

Figure 4.3 'The Score: Facts About Drugs'
Reproduced by permission of Crown Copyright

To sum up, there are several things to keep in mind. First, you are trying to provide clear, accurate and concise information. Second, note the 'weight' of the authority for whom you are writing. If you are writing for a government body such as a Health Authority or the Department of the Environment, or an official organisation, then you need to adopt a more authoritative stance. In addition, consider how specific your audience is, and how well you, as writer, know the audience.

Exercise 6

Finally, write your own 750 to 1,000-word booklet for the following question set by an exam board. (You could also turn this activity into an informative talk for radio.)

> Many people belong to organisations, clubs or societies and take a full part in their activities. These can range from large international or national organisations like Greenpeace, The Red Cross or Amnesty International to smaller local ones. They cover a huge range of interests and activities: charitable (Save the Children Fund, RSPCA, Scope, RSPB), community service (St John's Ambulance, The Samaritans, RAF and Army Training Corps), pressure groups (Friends of the Earth, Campaign for Real Ale) and leisure activities (Scouts/Guides, YWCA and YMCA, Duke of Edinburgh Award Scheme, local sports clubs, fitness centres or theatre groups). You will be able to think of many more examples and may even belong to one or more of these types of group yourself.
>
> However, people are often wary of joining, as they are unsure or apprehensive of just what is involved and what commitment they may be expected to make. To overcome this problem, many organisations produce a short booklet that is intended to inform prospective members in a friendly and approachable way about the activities or opportunities that are offered.
>
> Using your own knowledge and experience, write the first draft of such a booklet for an organisation, club or society. Be as specific as possible and think about the sort of information you yourself would like to have had before deciding whether to join.
>
> Remember that your intention is not to persuade people to join, but to help them reach an informed decision about whether this is the organisation or group for them.

SUMMARY

In this chapter we have explored:

- The way a personal, informed voice will lift a piece of informative writing
- The importance of humour
- The stylistic features of newspapers, magazines and radio news bulletins
- Approaches to reviews
- The importance of sound planning for interviews
- Establishing an authoritative tone for a public organisation
- The importance of clarity, brevity and accessibility for the chosen audience

WRITING TO INSTRUCT AND ADVISE

CHAPTER 5

INTRODUCTION

Instructional texts are often regarded rather condescendingly as straightforward and easy to write, and also mechanical, even . . . dull. These perceptions need not be true. Writing such texts can be challenging, interesting and illuminating. It is up to you!

THINK OF YOUR AUDIENCE

Exercise 1

'Radiotherapy 1' is a set of instructions for patients who have been discharged from hospital after treatment for cancer. 'Radiotherapy 2' is a more 'user-friendly' version of the same text. Compare both texts and note what changes have been made.

RADIOTHERAPY 1

1. Following X-ray or radium treatment whether by needles or superficial application, inflammation will occur. This process will be at its height in about *three* weeks and will thereafter subside and healing will follow.
2. During the reactionary inflammatory processes, it is necessary to keep the area clean and free from infection.
3. Bathe the whole area treated 3 or 4 times daily with salt and water – (a teaspoonful to the pint of cooled boiled water) – and apply the ointment provided. This can be done by spreading the ointment on clean sterilised gauze in a layer sufficiently thick to prevent sticking.
4. Before doing the dressing the hands should be washed and scrubbed in warm water, using a disinfectant soap.
5. The saline solution should be prepared freshly and each day in a special saucepan.
6. Avoid direct sunlight, excessive heat, or any other injury to the treated area.

continued

7. Use only the ointment provided, lanoline or Vaseline.
8. Do not hesitate to make an appointment to consult the medical officer in charge of the Radiotherapy Department should any untoward symptom develop.

RADIOTHERAPY 2

1. After you have X-ray treatment the area of skin affected will become inflamed. The inflammation will be at its worst after about three weeks. After that it will die down and the area will heal up.
2. While the inflammation continues you should take great care to keep the area clean and free from infection.
3. You should bathe the whole area 3 or 4 times every day with salt and water (a teaspoon to the pint of water that has been boiled and allowed to cool), and put on some of the ointment we have given you. You can do this by spreading the ointment on clean sterilised gauze, putting on a layer of ointment thickly enough to prevent sticking.
4. You should wash and scrub your hands with warm water and disinfectant soap before doing the dressing.
5. You should make a fresh salt solution every day keeping a saucepan especially for this purpose.
6. Take care to protect the treated area from direct sunlight, unusual heat or any kind of injury.
7. You should not apply any ointment except the one we have given you or lanoline or Vaseline.
8. If any unusual symptom should appear please make an appointment without delay to see the medical officer in charge of the Radiotherapy Department.

Suggestions for Answer

Most of you would probably sum up your general impression of the first passage by saying that its style seems formal, impersonal and detached. Of the second you are likely to note that, by comparison, it is less formal, more personal, warmer in tone, even more conversational.

The specific differences in language use have been set out in Table 5.1. (This has been done deliberately to show that there are different ways of presenting instructional writing.) The numbers in brackets refer to the paragraph in which the example occurs.

Table 5.1 Comparison of radiotherapy passages 1 and 2

	Radiotherapy 1	Radiotherapy 2
1	No first- or second-person pronouns Short imperatives ('Avoid' not 'You should avoid') 'The hands' (4)	Use of first- and second-person pronouns and possessive adjectives 'You' used throughout 'We' used twice 'Your' hands
2	Impersonal expressions which do not name the agent of a suggested action: It is necessary to keep (2) Inflammation will occur (1) Healing will follow (1)	Subject and active verb is a much commoner construction: You should take great care to keep Skin . . . will become inflamed The area will heal up
3	General use of passive verbs: This can be done (3) Hands should be washed (4) The saline solution should be prepared (5)	Use of active verbs: You can do this You should wash You should make
4	Vocabulary has examples of slightly unusual, near technical, Latinate expressions: Thereafter (1) Subside (1) Untoward (8) Apply (3) Processes (2)	Vocabulary is closer to that of 'everyday speech': After that Die down Unusual Put on
5	Style is generally terser; one word for several, adjective or participle instead of clause, etc.: Following (1) Cooled boiled water (3) Provided (7) During the (2) Daily (3) Healing	 After you have Water that has been boiled and allowed to cool We have given you While the . . . continues Every day The area will heal up
6	Others?	

WRITING TO INSTRUCT AND ADVISE 59

One key factor you need to decide is the stance you take as a writer. Using an appropriate tone for the targeted audience is a key issue in instructive writing. Look carefully at the following question set by an exam board on a subject very close to most students; in fact, its closeness makes it difficult to remain objective.

> Your school or college has decided to produce a short pamphlet (about 800 words) 'Preparing for Your First Interview' to be given to all post-16 students after the first year of their studies. These interviews may be for a university or college place or for employment.

You need a degree of semi-formality to communicate with your target audience but you also need to balance this with the innate seriousness of the subject. It would not be appropriate to create the impression that interviews are a good opportunity to cajole mum into buying you some new clothes, and if it's not a con, then it's a bit of a laugh. The most important clue in this respect is the reference in the question to 'your school or college'. These institutions are in one sense the real authors of the text. You need to imagine this pamphlet on display in Student Services or shown to universities or employers.

Exercise 2

Read the study guide 'Revision Blues?' written by a student as a piece of coursework (Figure 5.1). Now write your own instruction guide on 'How to Study: Tips and Exercises for GCSE Students'.

There are no suggestions for answer to this exercise.

REVISION BLUES?

REVISION BLUES?

Mountains of revision? Don't know where to start? G.C.S.E. revision seems so difficult at first and will always be tedious! BUT... Fear not my freaked out friend! This simple, step-by-step revision guide will guide you through your revision and help you to ace your exams! Remember...nothing easy is worthwhile and nothing worthwhile is easy!

'What should I revise?'

Some simple do's and don'ts to get you started.

DO'S
- ✓ Start early
- ✓ Use your syllabus as a guide
- ✓ Organise your notes clearly
- ✓ Re-read your notes
- ✓ Make a table of contents for your notes
- ✓ Practise past exam papers
- ✓ Draw diagrams
- ✓ Sketch mind maps

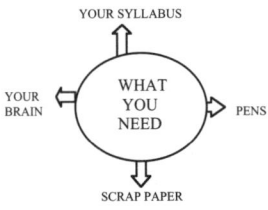

DIAGRAM: AN EXAMPLE OF A MIND MAP

DON'TS
- ✗ JUST read your notes. You need to read actively, with a pen in your hand to take notes, so that you take the work in.
- ✗ JUST work through questions. It is vital that you learn from your mistakes, so use practice questions and then re-read the parts that you did not understand.
- ✗ Forget to take a break! It is important to give your brain a break, so that your attention level is kept high when revising.

PICTURE: A STRESSED STUDENT NEARING EXAMS.

'Where is best to revise?'

It is important that you find a good place to revise, with no distractions so you can just get down to it.

Continued on page 62

Choose a place where;
▶ You won't be disturbed
▶ There is lots of space to spread out
▶ You can keep your notes organised
▶ You can keep scrap paper handy

'When is the best time to revise?'

The best time to revise is particular to you. Work when you feel active and fired up! It is important to MAKE time and a good idea to make a timetable like the one below.

	MONDAY	TUESDAY
4.00-4.15	SWIMMING	MATHS
4.15-4.30	SWIMMING	MATHS
4.30-4.45	SWIMMING	MATHS
4.45-5.00	BREAK	BREAK
5.00-5.15	FRENCH	HISTORY
5.15-5.30	FRENCH	HISTORY
5.30-5.45	FRENCH	HISTORY
5.45-6.00	HAVE TEA	HAVE TEA
6.00-6.15	HAVE TEA	HAVE TEA
6.15-6.30	ENGLISH	PIANO
6.30-6.45	ENGLISH	PIANO
6.45-7.00	WATCH TV	BREAK
7.00-7.15	WATCH TV	MUSIC
7.15-7.30	GRAPHICS	MUSIC
7.30-7.45	GRAPHICS	MUSIC
7.45-8.00	GRAPHICS	FINISH!

AN EXAMPLE TIMETABLE: USE COLOURS TO HIGHLIGHT THE DIFFERENT SUBJECTS.

Be organised, unlike Freddie the cartoon.

Set yourself targets for every revision session.

Top scientists have proven that people absorb more information in slots of 45 minutes of work with a 15-minute break.

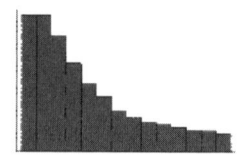

TIME SPENT REVISING GRAPH: SHOWING TIME AGAINST REVISION PERFORMANCE WITHOUT BREAKS.

This chart shows that without revision breaks performance deteriorates with time.

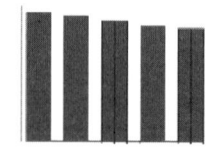

TIME SPENT REVISING GRAPH: SHOWING TIME AGAINST REVISION PERFORMANCE WITH BREAKS.

This chart shows that with regular breaks, (the white bars) peak performance is maintained.

Reward yourself with your favourite TV programme or a cream cake. Give yourself something to look forward to; revision *doesn't* have to be a total chore! So don't you forget it!

TIPS

1. Be realistic
2. Prioritise
3. Delete negative thinking,

REPEAT AFTER ME!
'I can do it!'
LOUDER.
'I CAN DO IT!'
I STILL CAN'T HEAR YOU!
'I CAN DO IT!'
Perfect!

Websites to help with your revision and come out with the A*s you deserve!
www.reviseit.co.uk
www.revisionguide.com
www.netrevision.co.uk

GOOD LUCK!

Figure 5.1 'Revision Blues?' study guide

WHAT ARE THE FEATURES OF AN INSTRUCTIVE TEXT?

Remember that instruction texts and information texts are often very closely linked. Many of the features identified in Chapter 4 apply here, and a number of texts cannot be rigidly defined as one or the other. A Health Department booklet about drugs may give information about the composition of drugs on one page and advise you how to detect signs of drug abuse on another. In your own writing you must decide what your primary purpose is and make sure that your text leans more to *telling* (for an informative text) or *telling how to* (an instructive text).

In your instructive text you should consider the following:

- Establish the organisation which has commissioned your booklet or leaflet clearly by name (and possibly also by logo or slogan to give your piece a professional look).
- More than any other purpose, instruction/advice demands a logical order and careful sequencing. This might mean adverbs of time: 'first', 'finally', 'then', bullets and subheadings. Paragraphs may be numbered, and they are usually short and separated by white space.
- Be precise in your choice of lexis. Be **denotative** rather than **connotative**, using literal meanings rather than those that may be ambiguous.
- **Imperatives** (command forms, such as 'add', 'mix', 'cook') are very common.
- Consider the use of insets (such as choice quotations). Use illustrations, graphs, diagrams and cartoons as appropriate to help your reader understand the point you are making. Vary font size, again to emphasise particular points.

HOW TO MAKE IT INTERESTING . . .

Even if you have done everything suggested so far, namely keeping your audience and the organisation behind your text in mind and reproducing the formal elements of textual organisation, it may not be enough to create a really interesting and therefore successful piece. Have you been adventurous, even taken risks? The challenge is to bring a sense of style and an original slant to your text, especially if it is a well-trodden area, such as advising against smoking.

The following are some examples of the way a 'No Smoking' text could be approached. One student adopted the title '1 + 1 = 2 . . . You + Cigarettes = Heart Problems, Lung Problems, Cancers, Smoker's Cough, Blackened Teeth, Blackened Lungs . . . ' and followed this with a logo (cigarette within a crossed out circle) and the slogan 'It All Adds Up!' for his leaflet for Year 6 students. A second adopted a Mills and Boon theme to start her leaflet. 'As they walked ankle deep in the delightfully warm water, he turned his bronzed profile towards her. She shut her eyes in anticipation, as he gently kissed her lips. "Euurgh! You're a smoker!" he cried in disgust.' A third created a Radio 4 programme. Against the 'bong' sound as at the start of *News at Ten* a roll-call of the famous who have succumbed to smoking-related illnesses was interspersed with advice from a medical expert and tips from peer group quitters.

MORE ADVICE THAN INSTRUCTION . . .

Many students will find that the quality of their writing will improve if they concentrate on offering advice. Personal experience is invaluable here. If you belong to the 'Can't Cook/Won't Cook' group, then writing 'Helpful Tips for Reluctant Cooks' may have a particular resonance. The same may be true for learner drivers. You are much more likely to have the right level of sympathy and understanding for others in the same boat. Computer phobia, bullying, eating disorders and relationship problems are a further selection of topics you may be able to address sympathetically and sensitively.

A very effective combination is what has been referred to as 'serious mindedness with a light touch'. It is worth studying a series of public health leaflets and booklets to get ideas for your own writing. There are a number of very helpful, sensitively produced ones available, with the 'light touch' suggested.

Exercise 3

Read the following extracts from two such texts. The first, Text A, was produced by *mentality* (note the lower case) and is entitled 'What do you think you are looking at?' (Figure 5.2). The second, Text B, is for the fpa (note the lower case and abbreviated form for the Family Planning Association). It is called 'Love S.T.I.NGS' (Figure 5.3).

Answer the following questions:

1. Comment on the audience that each is aimed at.
2. Comment on the differences in presentation and account for these.
3. What techniques are used to give advice sensitively?

There are no suggestions for answer to this exercise.

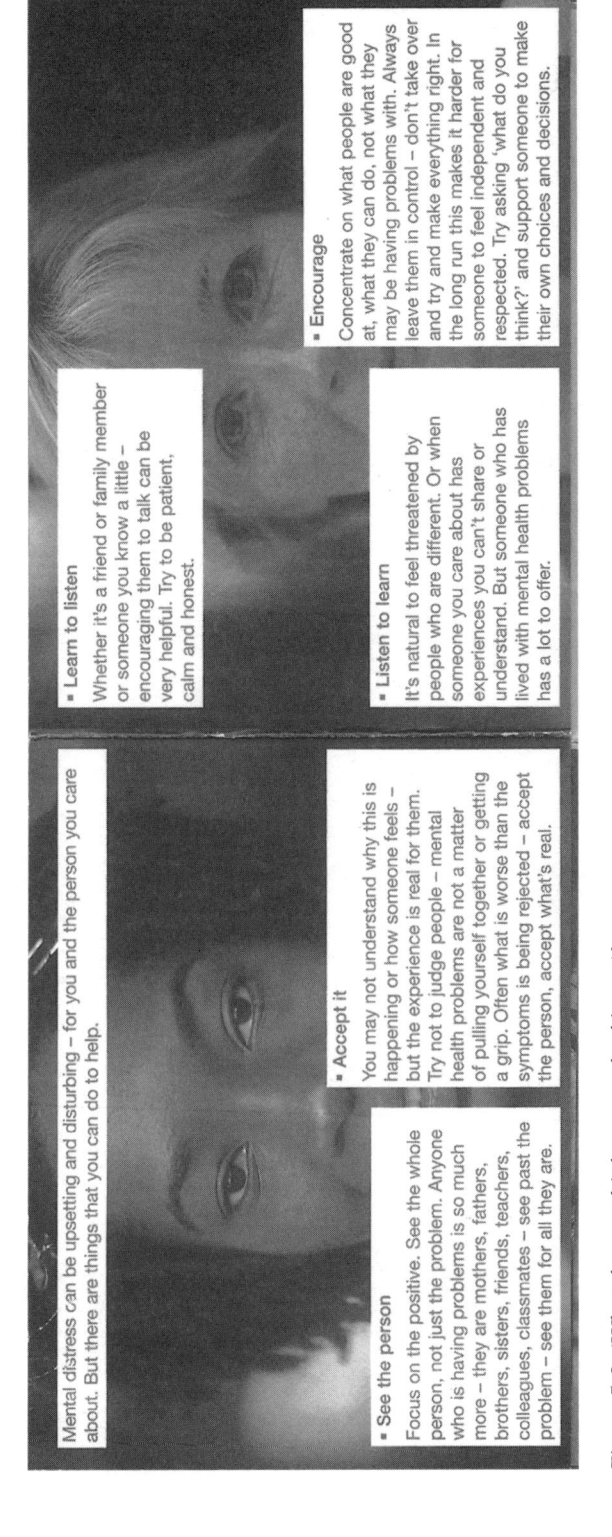

Mental distress can be upsetting and disturbing – for you and the person you care about. But there are things that you can do to help.

- **See the person**
  Focus on the positive. See the whole person, not just the problem. Anyone who is having problems is so much more – they are mothers, fathers, brothers, sisters, friends, teachers, colleagues, classmates – see past the problem – see them for all they are.

- **Accept it**
  You may not understand why this is happening or how someone feels – but the experience is real for them. Try not to judge people – mental health problems are not a matter of pulling yourself together or getting a grip. Often what is worse than the symptoms is being rejected – accept the person, accept what's real.

- **Learn to listen**
  Whether it's a friend or family member or someone you know a little – encouraging them to talk can be very helpful. Try to be patient, calm and honest.

- **Listen to learn**
  It's natural to feel threatened by people who are different. Or when someone you care about has experiences you can't share or understand. But someone who has lived with mental health problems has a lot to offer.

- **Encourage**
  Concentrate on what people are good at, what they can do, not what they may be having problems with. Always leave them in control – don't take over and try and make everything right. In the long run this makes it harder for someone to feel independent and respected. Try asking 'what do you think?' and support someone to make their own choices and decisions.

Figure 5.2 'What do you think you are looking at?'
Leaflet reproduced by permission of *mentality*

IF YOU THINK YOU COULD HAVE AN STI...

- Go to your local STI clinic or see a doctor
- Don't have sex until you are treated and given the all-clear
- Tell anybody you had sex with, so they can be tested and treated.

Hunt the clinic

Most large hospitals have a clinic. Names vary. Try looking in the phone book under:

- Sexual Health Clinic
- GUM (or Genitourinary Medicine) Clinic
- Sexually Transmitted Disease (or STD) Clinic
- Special Clinic

You can phone your local hospital switchboard.
Or phone the fpa or the National AIDS helpline (see back cover).

Free & confidential

Don't be put off visiting an STI clinic or a doctor because you think your family will be told. They won't. Nobody will be told without your agreement.
You can be any age – even if you are under the legal age of consent to sex, which is 16 (17 in Northern Ireland). And you don't even have to give your real name – you can make one up. And it's free.

Tests

The doctor at the clinic will normally give you a full sexual health check. This means looking at your genitals and mouth.
Some STIs can be diagnosed by sight e.g. pubic lice, genital warts.
Tests are carried out on blood and urine samples, or 'swabs' (cotton buds) are used to pick up samples of discharges or secretions.

Some tests can be completed while you wait. For others the results take up to 7 days. You will probably be asked to phone for some results (others, e.g. HIV, cannot be given over the phone). If you want an HIV test, ask. An HIV test is not automatic and will only be done after you have had a chance to discuss it with a health adviser or other member of staff.

Treatment

Most STIs can be completely cured if found early enough. Treatments can include:

- Antibiotics for bacterial infections such as Chlamydia. Be sure to take ALL the tablets.
- Viruses such as HIV and herpes cannot be cured, but treatment can relieve some symptoms.
- Lotions are used to treat crabs and scabies.

Advice

Anyone can ask to see a health adviser at a clinic to talk about relationships, sexuality, sexual problems or STIs.

Figure 5.3 'Love S.T.I.NGS'
Reproduced by kind permission of fpa from *Love S.T.I.NGS: A Beginner's Guide to Sexually Transmitted Infections*. Copyright © fpa 1999. Created for fpa by Comic Company. Illustrations by Ed Hillyer

Exercise 4

Now, put what you have learned into practice by answering the following question, set by an exam board. Before you embark on this task select at least one style model from your chosen magazine and note the double-page format carefully.

> From time to time, people find themselves having to plan and organise a special event, e.g. a birthday party, an engagement or wedding party, an anniversary, a religious celebration, a flat or house-warming party. You may have had experience of planning, or of being involved in, such an event.
>
> Sometimes popular magazines (e.g. *Family Circle, Esquire, GQ, Just 17, Marie Claire, Bella, Good Housekeeping*) feature ideas and advice on how to make these events enjoyable and smooth-running.
>
> You should write in a lively, interesting way, bearing in mind the double-page format. Choose a specific party or celebration for your article and indicate the magazine and audience for which you are writing.

There are no suggestions for answer to this exercise.

AND FINALLY, SOME ADVICE FROM AUNTY

One of the most successful ways to communicate with your reader is through the question-and-answer format. It is a comfortable and natural way to ask about and impart sensitive information. In the Health Education booklet *Women and Aids*, for example, all the advice and information is in the following format:

> *Q:* I think Steve my boyfriend once used drugs. Could he have HIV and what are the risks to me?
>
> *A:* If your boyfriend has ever shared drug injecting equipment then he might have HIV, the human immunodeficiency virus which causes Aids. HIV can be passed by sharing needles, syringes. . . . It is important for you both to talk about HIV and Aids so you can protect each other from infection.

The straightforward, practical advice given here is just what the 'agony aunts' provide in many papers and magazines in response to readers' questions.

Many of you may be avid readers of problem pages and find you can adopt the personal directness and sympathetic tone required. As a writing task, it is not in itself a sophisticated one but it does require knowledge of the conventions and, more importantly, a suitable tone of voice and an understanding of human psychology and emotions.

Start by collecting problem pages. Most have a title – 'Dear Claire/Veronica', 'You Ask Us', 'Mrs Mills Solves All Your Problems' – which suggests the nature of the task. Many then follow with the format of the open letter, without opening preamble or salutations at the end (that is, no 'Dear . . . ' or 'Yours sincerely'). However, the editor often titles the letters so that readers know what they are about: 'Money-grubbing' or 'Out for Revenge', for example. Many also warn that specifics cannot be addressed and end with 'No correspondence can be entered into'.

The style should bridge the immediate audience of the letter-writer and the wider audience of the readers of the magazine or newspaper. Try to establish an authoritative rapport. Your address should be personal and direct ('you') but exercise restraint. Empathising too deeply with a problem may seem alarmist and thus counter-productive, or overly gushing and annoying to the wider readership. The tone of the advice may be either sympathetic or critical, but, to be effective, should not be too harsh. Try to maintain a clear, lucid style which is neither over-complex nor too chatty. Using clichés is not necessarily a weakness here as many professional advice-givers introduce comforting and familiar phrases (e.g. 'Sticks and stones may break my bones but names will never hurt me', or 'Sleep on it'). Just don't bring in too many, and mention them in your commentary to show that you are aware of what you are doing. If you do draw on your own personal experience, always link it directly to the problem being discussed.

Exercise 5

The letter below, set by an exam board, focuses on a range of issues. The mother is expressing feelings of isolation and self-consciousness and is worried that her son is being teased at school. Write a response: this will need to achieve a balance between the problems of the mother and of the son, so it should be fuller and more detailed than such answers often are.

The following letter has been sent to a problem page in the magazine/newspaper that you read.

A Mother Writes About Her Son

I have always had problems getting on with people. It takes very little to have me hot under the collar with embarrassment at being shown up. If there is anything but friendly warmth in the way another person interacts with me, I feel put down. Small things, such as the confidence, attractiveness and intelligence of others, make me feel very inadequate. I know I am a worthy person, but it feels as though no one else thinks so.

> My main problem is that I see my nine-year-old son reliving my life with all its problems. He is fat (so am I) and self-conscious about it, and gets teased at school. His feelings are easily hurt and he cries too much. He takes normal boys' behaviour as offensive. They tend to run ahead and leave him, or don't include him in plans, or pick him for teams. Often he has no one to play with. I love him and try to build his self-esteem, but he is easily knocked back. He often seems depressed.
>
> I am so sad and guilty that I've inflicted this on him. How can I help him to solve his problems when I can't sort myself out?

There are no suggestions for answer to this exercise.

SUMMARY

In this chapter we have explored:

- The importance of establishing the right tone for your audience
- A range of tasks, noting degrees of complexity, from the mechanical to the challenging
- The features of an instructive text, including clarity, logic, sequencing, imperatives
- Seriousness with a light touch
- Ways of offering advice, including the problem page

VOICING ARGUMENT: THE ART OF PERSUASION

CHAPTER 6

INTRODUCTION

The media bombard us with spoken and written texts which cajole us to buy this or exhort us to believe and/or do that. There are plenty of style models available! So let us mention quickly genres of persuasion that by and large are not feasible, so you can avoid them and concentrate on those that *are* feasible. Exam boards have identified soap-box speeches to a crowd, live debates and phone-ins, and brochures for imaginary places as tasks to avoid – simply because they have no basis in reality. A letter to a newspaper may seem to be straightforward, but letter-writing is not in itself a challenging task, and letters for publication are generally characterised by their brevity. The discursive essay, the discussion of both sides of a controversial topic such as abortion or euthanasia, and a conclusion with your own point of view, has no place outside the academic work done in the classroom.

As has been said throughout this book, you can write powerful texts to be read or spoken if you keep your audience in mind, are aware of the characteristics of the genre you are writing for and have a real desire to say something. The last point, 'desire to say something', is particularly important when you are trying to persuade.

FRIENDS, ROMANS, COUNTRYMEN . . . PERSUASIVE SPEECH

Writing a persuasive speech is a deceptively difficult task, especially if 'speech' to you means a list of rhetorical devices and/or the speeches of orators such as Shakespeare's Mark Antony, Winston Churchill and Martin Luther King, which you may have studied in class. Some coursework, and even some exam answers, go wrong when students have studied a range of rhetorical techniques and try to find some topic that will allow them to be used. This often leads to unconvincing and overwritten speeches without a firm sense of audience or context.

When George Bush outlined the threat to an American audience before the invasion of Iraq in 2003, he used all the persuasive devices at his command because he *needed* the cooperation of the American people. Bush started his speech: 'Thank you for that very gracious and warm Cincinnati welcome. I'm honoured to be here tonight', because he wanted to flatter his listeners. He incorporated many rhetorical devices that rely on phonological effects, such as alliteration and lists of three – 'Iraq's eleven-year history of defiance, deception and bad faith' – and contrastive pairs – 'people everywhere prefer freedom to slavery, prosperity to squalor, self-government to the rule of terror and torture' – as well as balanced phrases: 'Saddam Hussein is harbouring terrorists and the instruments of terror, the instruments of mass death and destruction.' Finally, he employed repetition for effect, building to a climax: 'We will plan . . . we will act and we will prevail.' (Applause.)

These devices would sound artificial and the persuasion overdone in another context. If, for example, you were delivering a proposal for your community, perhaps for refurbishment of neglected amenities, or a sports event, gala, art exhibition, street theatre or children's event, then being able to argue a case in good, plain speech as well as feeling strongly about it is a real criterion for success.

However, you may achieve the emotional effect you are looking for with some of the following. The examples are taken from the same Bush speech.

- *Emotive language*: 'grave threat', 'horrible poisons', 'homicidal dictator'
- *Hyperbole*: 'massive stockpile . . . capable of killing millions', and superlatives: 'first and greatest benefit'
- *Metaphor*: 'arsenal of terror', 'using murder as a tool of terror and control'
- *Euphemism*: 'We cannot wait for the final proof – the smoking gun [weapons of mass destruction] – that could come in the form of a mushroom cloud [the nuclear bomb]'
- *Inclusive address and direct address*: '*I* want to share those discussions with *you*'
- *Rhetorical questions*: 'Why be concerned now?' (Be careful that you do not assault the reader with a list of rhetorical questions)

Exercise 1

Read the following script of an actual speech which was given to a women's organisation by an A Level student.

Identify and comment on the features used to engage the reader's attention.

The Female Nation, United We Stand

Once upon a time, there lived lots of little girls, destined to grow up and find the man of their dreams and have their own baby girls, who in turn would find their one true love and boast about their own little darlings.

Once upon a time, there was a young girl who dreamed of a fairy-tale wedding with a handsome prince.

Once upon a time . . . but not any more.

A prince and a palace, diamonds and pearls; letting our long, flowing hair cascade down the side of a locked tower so the brave knight can rescue us; having a magical godmother who can turn our tattered shoes into slippers of glass. I'd settle for turning my Nine Wests into Manolo Blahniks, but let's face it, life just isn't that kind. We've all been taught what to wish for, but in the twenty-first century, reality rarely delivers.

Fairy tales adhere to all the stereotypes that generations of women have struggled to overcome. We verbally slaughter the man who judges us by our looks. We want to be judged by our minds not our appearance. We want to be treated the same as men, as equals.

Or do we? In the rush of post-feminist values, one begs to wonder why we insist we want to be judged exclusively by our personalities and intellectual worth, when in fact, men are themselves becoming increasingly obsessed with vanity – their own appearance.

More disturbing is what has become of our dream of being swept off our feet by the noble stranger. Fantasising at the idea of a romantic encounter with a mythical husband-to-be, we realise that none of the genuine prospective candidates are the Princes or 'Charmings' we'd hoped for. In reality, our handsome princes are not rescuing us from 'fairy-tale' scenarios. We haven't got men unlocking the tower that we have been confined to by the fire-breathing dragon.

Mr Tall Dark and Handsome isn't sweeping anyone away on the foundations of their academic achievements and commendable ethics, is he? How many men have insisted that they are always first attracted to a woman because of her personality? The Jennifer Aniston look-alike he stares at every day displays a natural charisma and charm that is apparent, even though he's never actually talked to her. The supplement of his *FHM* was once titled 'The 100 brainiest women in the world', only to be inadvertently replaced with 'sexiest'. Not.

It's not enough to look in the mirror and feel truly satisfied with the way you look, if nobody else appreciates it. If we want to be valued solely on our inner qualities, then why do we spend an hour at the gym in our lunch break? Why do we spend an entire week's pay on the newest Dior creation and continue to throw our money away on the products of Donna Karen and Ruby Hammer? After years of telling ourselves that we're doing it for us, it's time to admit that we're not. Not just for us.

Burning our bras, once deemed to be the shackles of dependence, has supposedly released a wave of equality. No man should receive a higher salary than his female counterpart. No husband should treat his wife as his slave. In spite of this, disparity still occurs. However, now we're even losing the right to be honoured publicly as the gentle sex. Why aren't men allowed to open

continued

our doors for us? Why can't they stand when we enter a room? Do we really find this sexist, or are we just cutting off our noses to spite our own faces?

The pretence has gone on long enough. It's not offensive to judge women on how they look. It's a cue for the facially challenged to propel one of their better qualities. If we are genuinely trying to encourage a politically correct handling of the perception of the female society, then we need to consider both sides of the coin.

I don't condemn the feminist view entirely. None the less, demanding a disregard for some of our nicer traditionalist values can have adverse effects. The reason we aren't treated exactly like men is quite simple. We are not men. And to be completely honest, I'm often glad I'm not!

Beauty is an attribute that should be celebrated as aptitude is. The female is an amazing entity and while we all strive for appreciation on a higher level, we can take pleasure in the more superficial admiration while we wait.

All women like a compliment. Every girl appreciates an admiring look and everybody wants to feel beautiful. There's never been anything wrong with that and it's nothing to be ashamed of. So, while we all hope to be treated like a man, we should bask in the glory of being a woman and celebrate the beauty and power of the female nation. United we stand!

Suggestion for Answer

Here is part of the student's own commentary.

The piece begins with a clichéd opening, typically reserved for use in fairy tales: '*Once upon a time.*' This is unexpected and immediately grabs the attention of the audience. The first three paragraphs cohere lexically, due to the repetition of 'Once upon a time'. I have specifically created a pattern of three as this is a typical device used to instil an idea. This section ends with 'not any more', clarifying that the topic about to be discussed is not a fairy tale. This reverses the reader's expectations.

I have used direct, but inclusive appeal, 'Letting our long, flowing hair' . . . near the beginning of the piece, immediately introducing a relationship with the audience and including them.

Deliberate lexical choices create specific effects. *A 'mythical husband-to-be*' is not very politically correct, where the word 'partner' would have been more appropriate. However, this choice is an 'old-fashioned' touch, highlighting just how outdated the idea of a 'fairy-tale' lifestyle is. 'Boast about their own little darlings', creates a similar effect, reflecting the traditional attitudes of parents possessing their daughters.

I hope I have included humour in my speech. '*I'd settle for turning my Nine Wests into Manolo Blahniks.*' Comparing the act of buying footwear with a dream of having a fairy godmother adds comedy, lowering the register of formality and creating a light-hearted style. I have also played on the assumption that my audience would be familiar with both labels, Manolo Blahnik being a top fashion designer and Nine West being a brand found more commonly on the high street. This makes the speech more personal, as an insider reference is being used.

The speech is designed to challenge the thinking of the audience. A lot of opinions are expressed and these, particularly when linked with rhetorical questions such as '*Do we really find this sexist, or are we just cutting off our noses to spite our own faces?*' enable the audience to rethink their views. A secondary purpose of entertaining complements that of the primary purpose to persuade. The audience is more likely to consider the issues being raised if they are enjoying the way in which they are delivered.

Some of the sentences are incomplete constructions: '*Not just for us.*' This is deliberate; as the piece is to be spoken, it does not adhere to the conventions of written language. Various phonological features such as alliteration are also used: '*A prince and a palace, diamonds and pearls.*' The repetition of the plosive consonant adds emphasis to what is being said.

Furthermore, sections of the speech could be further emphasised through the use of appropriate intonation. For example, one paragraph is particularly sarcastic: '*"the 100 brainiest women in the world", only to be inadvertently replaced with "sexiest". Not.*' I have added the word 'Not' at the end of this sentence to qualify that the previous sentences were, in fact, mocking a stereo-typed male quality. However, the use of this ending might not be necessary if a sarcastic tone was used.

I have exploited the widespread familiarity with fairy-tale stories and values adopted by different people and groups. This speech would be neither effective nor appropriate in a culture where such values do not exist. The speech relies on assumed familiarity with such terms as '*Fairy godmother*' – and therefore is only applicable to culture-specific audiences.

The use of visual aids would add to the effectiveness of the piece overall. Various images could be projected on to a screen during specific sections with the use of an overhead projector or a presentation software package and computer.

Another spoken task that allows you to think in terms of a 'real' audience is a presentation to a school assembly. Since schools are required to instruct their students in values and civic responsibilities, there is strong demand for presentations with a generally moral message. Traditionally suitable topics for, say, 13- to 15-year-olds are bullying, shoplifting, truancy and experimenting with drugs. You might also consider exploring aspects of human experience such as being accepted for who you are, betraying a confidence, being misunderstood, disappointment or failure, envy or revenge.

Observe the following pointers:

- Keep your audience in mind and remember that they are a *listening* audience. Record your speech, possibly with a real audience.
- Your text needs to be independent of you as the writer, so be careful about writing/speaking about yourself. 'Confessional' writing can be too intense or embarrassing, or can come across as whingeing, if you are being told constantly how the narrator feels.
- You may wish to borrow from different genres. For example, you might start and finish with direct, persuasive address but include narrative fiction, diary entries, fables or cautionary tales, elements of case histories and factual accounts.
- A telling detail can be far more compelling than an over-insistent persuasive tone.

Advertising campaigns provide the opportunity to write interesting, imaginative and focused writing if you are familiar with the techniques and idioms of modern selling. Radio advertising especially calls for skill, invention and a lot of discipline. The radio commercial needs to be tightly packaged. Your script needs to be brief because you will have perhaps thirty seconds to convey the key message and also to fix the brand name and the desired image of the product in the listener's mind. It must also have immediate impact, with perhaps a catchy jingle, multiple voices, a mini-drama that can be developed (cue TV's Nescafé Gold Blend couple), and must have lively dialogue for a listening audience. Think carefully of the aural perspective; you will need to include sound effects, music and the mixing of these, such as a slogan repeated against the background of a theme tune.

Many students produce very good multimedia campaigns, such as a short radio advertisement accompanied by printed texts (e.g. a mail shot, a poster and/or an advertising feature). This is a good idea, given the fact that in the real world advertisers want to create maximum impact as briefly as they can, so writing enough to fulfil the requirements of coursework or an exam might otherwise be a problem. However, these do need to constitute a single submission and in order to do that you must keep in mind the same primary purpose and audience. Make sure that you maintain continuity, with echoes of the words or visual elements repeated appropriately for the different media.

Exercise 2

Now answer the following question:

> A major clothing manufacturer wishes to break into the younger market and has decided to begin by concentrating on the production and marketing of a range of outdoor leisure wear for both men and women. The company is willing to devote a sizeable budget to an advertising campaign for these clothes. It wants the campaign to have the same theme and image running throughout and intends to use all the available media – print, poster, radio, TV and cinema.
>
> The company has given you complete freedom to decide on a suitable name and image for the clothing and a theme for the advertisements. You must write the following:
>
> 1. The scripts for a series of three or four short, linked radio advertisements on a popular music station
> 2. The text for a single advertisement to be published in magazines with a wide readership in the 18 to 30 age group
>
> Write about 750 words in total for exam practice, and up to 1,000 words for coursework, dividing them suitably between the two tasks. Use an appropriate layout for the radio scripts (remind yourself of the conventions by rereading Chapter 3) and indicate the layout of the magazine advertisement.

There are no suggestions for answer to this exercise.

PERSUASION IN PRINT

If a persuasive speech relies on the intonation and tone of the speaking voice for some of its colour and emphasis, so persuasive writing, especially in coursework tasks, will benefit from care taken with graphology. The way you lay out your material, the use of typographical variation (different typefaces, capitalisation, italics, emboldening), as well as logos, slogans, cartoons, pictures and colour, will influence your reader.

There are a range of possible genres and approaches you may take in order to write persuasive prose, many of which have been covered in previous chapters. For example, the leaflet and (junk mail) letter become persuasive if they are presented in an emotive way as part of a charity appeal. The feature article or cautionary tale mentioned earlier in this chapter which exhorts the reader to alter a habit or viewpoint, buy something, or support someone or something, is persuasive.

However, the best writing doesn't obviously or insistently promote a cause. A hook to engage the reader, careful use of emotive language, variety, liveliness and a light touch will win your reader over much more effectively.

Exercise 3

Read the following 'recipe'.

This is the opening of an Amnesty International appeal. The contrast between the usual domesticity of the context and the reality, and the intertextuality of the title, provide a very effective shock tactic in Amnesty's campaign to stop torture.

> ### Mexican Chilli Con Carnage
>
> For this you need one 18-year-old girl
> And several policemen.
>
> **Method**:
>
> Blindfold girl. Rape. Apply electric shocks to nipples. Push head into a vat of water. Force carbonated water and chilli powder up nose. Beat till tender.
>
> Reprinted by permission of Amnesty International

Now write your own short persuasive text using an unexpected genre or tone. Decide whether you want to be deliberately formal, sarcastic, familiar or tongue in cheek. Whatever you decide, the intention is to expose vice or folly or to challenge assumptions, by jolting the reader's expectations without openly urging the reader to your point of view.

Here are further examples to help get you started. You might write a cautionary tale for teenagers in the style of Roger Hargreaves' 'Little Miss' and 'Mr Men' children's series, or adopt the device a TV critic used recently, of 'previewing' a tape which arrived without a sound-track. He was able to poke fun at a popular makeover programme by suggesting that this must be a pilot for a romantic comedy set in a leafy suburb!

Exercise 4

Now that you have practised adopting a critical stance and a lively, confrontational address, answer the following exam board question:

> The national newspaper that you read has started a series of features entitled 'Overrated?' in its weekend magazine section. Each week a contributor chooses a celebrated example of popular culture and presents an alternative

viewpoint, which challenges its popular acclaim. Possible examples include TV or radio programmes, books, films, types of music, sporting activities and events.

- Write an article on one example of popular culture for inclusion in the series (700 to 800 words for exam practice and up to 1,500 words for coursework).
- State the newspaper for which you are writing. The tone should be lively, but authoritative, and the style in keeping with that of your chosen newspaper.
- Suggest your own headline and subheadings, but if you are doing this for an exam do not concern yourself with layout or the inclusion of pictures.

THE ISSUE OF PLAGIARISM

Chapter 1 mentioned the importance of writing your own original texts and being able to demonstrate that you haven't copy-shadowed your material. This chapter has suggested alternative ways of making your texts effective and putting your own individual stamp on your material.

However, there will be tasks that you choose whose effectiveness lies in their very familiarity to the target audience and the fact that their features are recognised and expected. Some charity campaigns fall into this category. So, how can you get around this problem?

One student's mock campaign for the charity Shelter consisted of a mail shot including a leaflet and a personalised letter. By choosing a dual-genre submission he immediately took the opportunity to display awareness of different types of writing, and thus lessened the charge of plagiarism. The leaflet (not produced here) had its own slogan 'Who will you help this Christmas?' followed by the catchphrase 'Last year over 1180 people were sleeping on the streets of Britain. This Christmas you could make it 1179.'

However, even with the additions already mentioned, the effectiveness of such a campaign lies in the fact that it must seem credible for its known organisation; after all, the student took care to identify Shelter as a 'real life organisation that aims to combat homelessness across Britain, regularly sending out such campaigns to householders'. Part of the effectiveness of the student's original submission was the closeness of the graphological and discourse features to real Shelter letters.

Read the extracts from the letter and the commentary following, and identify the features that show this is not simply 'copying'.

For the past 30 years we have been raising money to help those sleeping on the streets – not just issuing handouts, but also putting people <u>in houses, in training, and in employment</u>. However, we can only continue to do this with the help of people like you. If you could give just <u>£25 per year</u> – that's less than <u>7p per day</u> – then you will help us continue the fight against homelessness.

<u>Jacob, 34</u>

Jacob was 17 when he first started sleeping on the streets. He'd finished school, and after a turbulent home life decided to move into a flat with some friends. Within a short time, his friends were using the flat as a place to deal drugs and Jacob realised it was time to go. With no money and no accommodation, no one wanted to know, and Jacob found himself sleeping rough.

'I spent ten years sleeping rough, on and off. It's not good, it's frightening, and some of my friends bullied me.'

After being treated for depression, Jacob found a bed at the Millennium Plus project, run by Shelter, and was given advice on money, alcohol, drugs and housing. He later moved into a care home which 'has its disadvantages, but is better than sleeping on the streets'.

By giving just <u>7p per day</u>, you can pay for a Shelter worker to rehouse people just like Jacob, and help them to secure a future.

Commentary

This piece of coursework consists of a charity campaign, split into two sections: an informative, persuasive leaflet and a persuasive letter – both to be mailed to householders in the same envelope. The charity involved, Shelter, is a real-life organisation that aims to combat homelessness across Britain, regularly sending out such campaigns. The campaign is aimed at the middle-class, middle-aged couple or person who often has more disposable income and so is more willing to donate to charity.

The letter is intended to be the first item to be read and one of the immediate persuasive features I have included is the use of the second-person pronoun 'you', especially the construction 'people like you', to flatter the reader and make him feel that he has been specially selected to receive this mailing.

A large part of the letter is devoted to a real-life case study, adapted from the Shelter website (www.shelter.org.uk), which demystifies people's preconceptions of how people become homeless. This should make the reader more willing to donate, as they can see that their money will not be wasted. I have also used figures and percentages obtained from the Shelter website.

The rhetorical features of a list of three (in houses, in training and in employment), repetition and underlining give emphasis and show what *can* be done and the determination of the charity to do it. Additional emphasis may be seen in the donation amount: '£25 per year . . . 7p per day' as this is the main point of the campaign – to donate money. The conversion of £25 per year into 7p per day serves seemingly to lower the cost to the individual; 7p per day is a pittance for the average audience member.

Suggestions for Answer

The student individualises his letter by creating a case study, which he highlights in his commentary: 'A large part of the letter is devoted to a real-life case study, adapted from the Shelter website.' He names his subject, provides him with characteristic dialogue and creates a convincing history for him.

Importantly, he gives credibility to his text by identifying the research he has done. He has adapted his material from the Shelter website, for which he gives a reference. His use of facts and figures is similarly authenticated.

He comments on stylistic choices made, such as the use of the second-person pronoun 'you' to 'make [the reader] feel as if he had been specially selected to receive this mailing', and the use of lists of three, repetition and underlining to add emphasis to the persuasive message. He makes it clear that he understands the effect such devices have on the reader.

SUMMARY

In this chapter we have explored:

- The features of persuasive language
- The pros and cons of speech writing – avoiding artificial rhetoric
- Multimedia campaigns, including radio advertising
- The importance of audience, genre and graphology
- Ways of avoiding an over-insistent tone
- Ways of creating a new text, not copying an existing one

HOW TO GET STARTED CHAPTER 7

Since this book started with the commentary, it seems only fitting to end with some ideas that you can draw on to give you inspiration. Often inspiration can come from the most unlikely sources. Songwriter Phil Bird (see Chapter 2) always keeps a notebook with him to jot down ideas. He says these come from all sorts of places, the news, novels, other songs and personal experiences. The author Françoise Sagan said, 'I have to start to write to have ideas.'

So, how do you get going? Try some creative starters.

- Write down in a scrap-book interesting phrases and ideas that you hear or read.
- Assemble a random group of objects (e.g. a postcard, a rusty nail, an oriental lamp, a polished stone) and weave a history for one or more of them.
- Create a persona for one of the following names: Arvon Hanneman, Steven Runkle, Fil Edwardes. (Why might Fil write his or her name with 'F' not 'Ph'?)
- Write down five sounds that you can hear, then list the things you associate with those sounds.
- Make a list of your interests and/or pet hates. You may surprise yourself with the possibilities. Don't forget that Joanne Harris wrote her novel *Chocolat* based on her passion for chocolate.
- Many students feel comfortable about writing an informative text, but lack inspiration or feel that the area they are interested in has been covered extensively already. Flick through some more 'informative' magazines for ideas. For example, opposite is the Contents page of a recent edition of *Driveon*, the magazine for new drivers (Figure 7.1). Notice the range of possibilities, many connected only loosely to motoring. There are ideas here that could be adapted for stories, as well as informative, persuasive and instructive writing.
- Become a collector of all sorts of trifles: pick up leaflets from gyms, doctors' surgeries, restaurants and supermarkets for information for a 'Guide to . . . ' or 'A Day in the Life of . . . ' or 'In the Psychiatrist's Chair'. Paste amusing and/or thought-provoking cuttings in a folder as well. Again, they might become stories, playscripts, leaflets or magazine double-page spreads.
- Visit your local tourist office or any tourist agency and collect brochures. Read other travel writers' accounts. (Bill Bryson's *Notes from a Small Island* is particularly witty and accessible.) Use plans you may be making for your own intended holiday to help you, or draw on experience you already have to write a persuasive article for fellow travellers, an advice guide or a travelogue.

Contents

6 Accelerator
The world of motoring – it's a very strange planet. Plus you can WIN a new Renault Mégane with Michelin

14 Designer Cars
The people who design the best suits in the world aren't always the best people to design your cars. But they are entertaining!

16 Act Smart
The New Driver's Act affects every driver – and that means you

20 Channel Hopping
Now you have the freedom of the road – so why not take the open road to Europe?

26 Drug Driving
Driving mixes with a lot of things – friends, family, work, sunshine – but it definitely doesn't mix with drugs

28 'P' Plates
Find out the benefits of the green P Plate

30 Round and Round
Your new car is already made from many recycled components – which ones?

36 Pay Per Drive
The new company car tax is worth understanding

40 The Idea Olympics
Have they really invented a car powered by hamsters?

42 You Have Half a Second Left
An accident takes no time, but those few seconds could be your last

46 Paper Chase
Paperwork is boring, but it might be a legal requirement

50 Gear!
Manual, full auto and everything in between – there's a lot going on when you shift that gear lever

52 Get Ahead
Advanced driving benefits everyone, especially you

54 Zero Emissions
It's the holy grail, and manufacturers are moving closer to ensuring that the car is far less of a planet polluter

58 Speed
It thrills, it kills – here's what your right leg's up to

Driveon 2003

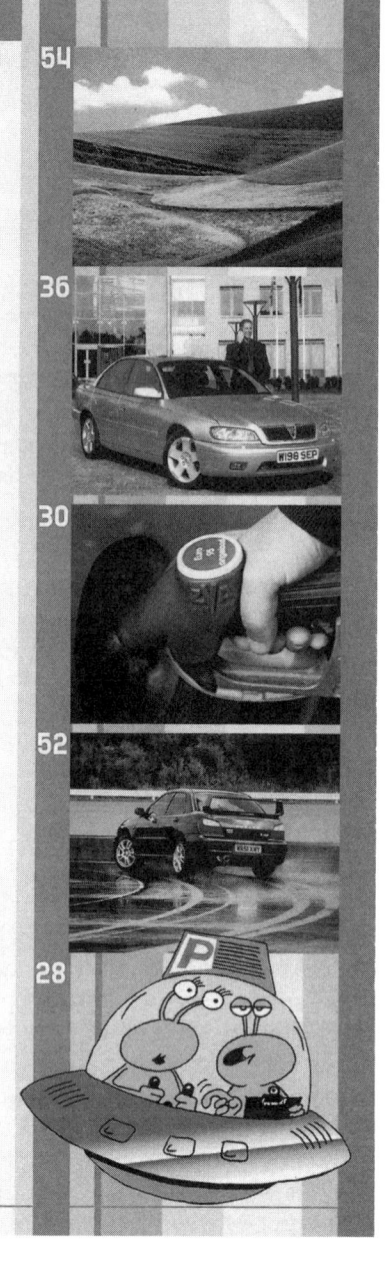

Figure 7.1 *Driveon* Contents page, 2003
Reproduced by permission of the Driving Standards Agency

Once started on at least some of the suggestions above, you will, with a bit of luck, wish to take your writing further. Apart from working for exams, you can enter writing competitions, get work experience in a newspaper office and/or get involved in writing online. But be warned: once you have discovered your own particular voice as a writer, you may find it hard to stop!

SUGGESTIONS FOR ANSWER

CHAPTER 2, EXERCISE 4

Bridget's objections seem quite reasonable, initially; she is not a close friend or relative, but her next objection is amusingly trivial: she would have to miss both *Blind Date* and *Casualty*. There is a contrast with Bridget's own diary shorthand, with **elliptical**, non-standard sentences: 'Seem to remember from childhood am supposed to reply in same oblique style' and the highly formal invitation written in the third person. Bridget mocks the rigidity of the format by employing a **euphemism**: 'like calling the ladies' powder room the toilet'.

The real humour lies in the increasingly exaggerated drafts of her reply. Notice that Bridget starts with the stated intention of declining the invitation 'clearly and firmly' and the first draft does just that. In successive drafts emotive language, exaggeration and complex word order (syntax) indicate her increasing frustration with the whole process. (The reader has been told earlier that she makes fourteen attempts at drafting the reply.) The climax is the ludicrous scenario of Bridget being unable to attend because she has 'topped herself', an inappropriately colloquial expression after the conventional formality of 'it is with great regret', because of her 'distress' at not being able to accept the invitation.

CHAPTER 3, EXERCISE 6

Brent tries to portray how popular and switched on he is through his **paralanguage**. This is reflected in the stage directions. He 'grins excitedly' when pointing out the 'flat Eric' doll impaled on a coat stand and 'waits for a big laugh'. Everything he does is exaggerated and inappropriate. He 'scoots' over to Gareth to make the introductions and is 'unfazed' when he is met by bewilderment from Ricky.

Brent's language shows that he is pompous, self-centred, loud and brash. Notice how many exclamations there are. 'Ooh, careful, watch this one! Woh, woh, woh, woh,' and he hijacks Gareth's introduction by pointing to himself and reinforcing the fact that Gareth is assistant to him, the Regional Manager. His language is dated: 'Slow down, you move too fast' and 'Solomon's here' would be unintelligible to someone not familiar with music popular more than twenty years ago or with biblical references. His attempt at a suggestive joke is again inappropriate and unnecessarily offensive: 'Gareth's my right-hand man, immediately beneath me . . . ooh, as an actress said to a bishop! No, he's not. I'm not. . . . '

Gareth supports Brent in his smugness with a ghastly dual act, in which they add to each other's utterances: 'It was just a wreck' . . . 'Respray' . . . 'Built it himself . . . ' This and the fact that he has photos all ready to produce and *recoils in horror* at the sight of the practical joke, which, tellingly has been played on him *again*, indicate that he is a pedantic jobsworth who is the butt of the office joker.

Tim actually says and does little in this scene but his contributions are significant. He at least talks *to* Ricky, not *at* him in his 'Hello, alright?', and putting the stapler inside the jelly is a sign that he is trying to get a point across. Why is he trying to wind Gareth up? Is he making a protest against an environment he hates?

CHAPTER 4, EXERCISE 5

The sentence types are short declaratives. The paragraphs are also short and text blocks are broken up with white space. Sequential numbering in Text A and subheadings in Text B add to the clarity.

The mode of address in Text A is a direct, second-person address ('How *you* think'), whereas Text B is more distanced ('*People* take drugs to make *them*').

In Text A, the green dots on the yellow numbers look childlike and the title looks handwritten. Key points are in bold. Red and black have long been associated with danger and diseases and the swirl of colours on the other side of Text B may reflect the hallucinogenic properties of some of the drugs. The small symbols represent the drugs being considered. The headings are capitalised and are a different colour.

Text A has straightforward lexis and any difficult terms are glossed ('illegal – against the law'). The use of second-person address, the short declaratives and the graphology suggest a young audience. Text B uses field-specific, scientific and Latinate lexis ('analgesics', 'alkyl nitrates', 'distorting'), and although each group is explained, the third-person address, overall high level of the language and the specific and wide-ranging 'drug files' indicate that this text is aimed at an older audience.

GLOSSARY

Alliteration The repetition of similar consonant sounds in a sequence of words (usually beginning with the same sound)

Assonance A sequence of repeated vowel sounds

Bathos Lapse in mood from the elevated to the trivial

Cohesion A term which refers to the words and grammatical structures which provide links across clause and sentence boundaries so that a text reads in a logically connected and coherent way

Coinage The creation of a new word out of existing elements

Collocation/collocate The way certain words frequently appear together, often in a certain order

Complex sentence A sentence made up of a main part and subordinate parts

Connotation/connote The associations a word implies or suggests

Contradiction A statement that is at variance or conflicts with the facts

Declarative A sentence type; a statement or assertion

Denotation/denote Whereas connotation looks at the personal or emotional association aroused by a word, denotation limits meaning to the thing or action or quality to which a word refers

Discourse structure The way texts cohere (see **cohesion** above) and the ways in which readers recognise this

Dramatic monologue A form where one speaker is addressing an audience

Ellipsis/elliptical The omission of a word or words from a sentence

Emotive The emotional and persuasive content of a use of language

Euphemism The use of a mild word or phrase instead of one which is unpleasant or offensive

Filler Words or sounds that fill up pauses in speech

Genre Types of texts. It can refer broadly to such things as poetry, prose, drama, but also more specifically to types of text within these broad areas, such as crime fiction or feature articles

Grammar The study of sentence structure, especially syntax and word classes (noun, verb)

Graphology The visual aspects of text, including layout and images

Hyperbole Emphatic exaggeration for effect

Imperative A form of command

In medias res Starting a narrative by plunging into the middle of the action

Intertextuality The way in which a text echoes or refers to another text (e.g. a billboard for an insurance company read 'Honey, they've shrunk the mortgage' after the film *Honey, I've Shrunk the Kids*)

Irony The gap between what is said and what is meant

Journalese A term used to describe words that come to be associated with newspapers

Minor sentence A 'sentence' which lacks one of the necessary elements (e.g. a main verb or a subject)

Mode The sort of text (e.g. spoken or written)

Naïve narrator The narrator is unaware that the audience is able to put a very different interpretation on the story being told (see **irony** above)

Omniscient The third-person, 'all-seeing' point of view

Onomatopoeia The sounds of the words used reflect their meaning (e.g. *buzz*)

Paralanguage Gestures and facial expressions which contribute to the meanings in speech

Phonology The study of the way sound operates within language

Plagiarism Borrowing thoughts and ideas and passing them off as original

Point of view The angle from which the events are seen. This may be first person (*I, we*), second person (*you*) or third person (*s/he, they*)

Pronoun Words which stand instead of nouns (e.g. *I, you*)

Prosodic features Aspects of the use of the voice such as rhythm, speed, pitch and emphasis

Pun A play on two or more possible meanings of a word

Register The level of formality of a text, and the vocabulary associated with it (e.g. legal terms)

Satire The use of ridicule, irony or sarcasm to expose folly or vice, or to lampoon an individual

Semantic field A grouping of words with related or similar meanings

Semantics The study of meaning

Sociolect The distinctive vocabulary and grammatical constructions used by an identifiable social group

Stream of consciousness A style of writing: random, unstructured thoughts and impressions of the narrator

Syntax The way sentences are constructed; word order

Tone The 'voice' in which the writer 'speaks', which may be humorous, serious, bullying and so on

Traditional structure Usually four-part, which includes situation, complication, crisis and resolution

Related titles from Routledge

Inter text

Edited by **Angela Goddard**, Manchester Metropolitan University, UK and **Adrian Beard**, University of Newcastle upon Tyne, UK.

The *Intertext* series has been specifically designed to meet the needs of contemporary English Language Studies. The core book, *Working with Texts*, is the foundation text that provides an introduction to language analysis. It is complemented by a range of 'satellite' titles that provide students with hands-on practical experience of textual analysis through special topics. They can be used individually or in conjunction with *Working with Texts*.

Each *Intertext* satellite title is:

- highly interactive, offering a range of task-based activities both for class use and self study
- written in a clear, accessible, user-friendly style with a full glossary
- fully illustrated with a variety of real language texts: literary texts, memos, signs, advertisements, leaflets, speeches, conversations

---

Available at all good bookshops
For ordering and further information on the Intertext series please visit:
www.routledge.com/rcenters/linguistics/series/intertext.html

The English Studies Book
An Introduction to Language, Literature and Culture: Second Edition
Rob Pope

'Innovative, imaginative, resourceful and full of surprises, the second edition of *The English Studies Book* continues to be an outstanding introduction to all aspects of the study of English literature and culture.'
Robert Eaglestone, *Royal Holloway, University of London*, UK

The English Studies Book is designed to support students and teachers working across the full range of courses in language, literature and culture. Combining the functions of study guide, critical dictionary and text anthology, it has rapidly established itself as a core text on a wide variety of degree programmes, nationally and internationally.

This new edition takes full account of current changes in the subject while maintaining the authority, accessibility and flexibility so valued by users of the first edition. Revised and updated throughout, features include:

- A new prologue addressing changes and challenges in English Studies today
- Substantial entries on over 100 key critical and theoretical terms
- Practical introductions to all the major theoretical approaches, with new sections on aesthetics, ethics, ecology and sexuality
- A rich anthology of literary and related texts from Anglo-Saxon to Afro-Caribbean, with fresh selections representing the sonnet, haiku, slave narratives and science fiction, and with additional texts by Elizabeth Barrett Browning, Charles Darwin, Ian McEwan, Margaret Atwood, Amy Tan and others
- Handy frameworks and checklists for close reading, research, essay writing and other textual activities, including use of the Internet

The English Studies Book is a comprehensive and invaluable reference tool for anyone interested in the study of English language, literature and culture.

0–415–25709–3
0–415–25710–7

eBooks

eBooks – at www.eBookstore.tandf.co.uk

A library at your fingertips!

eBooks are electronic versions of printed books. You can store them on your PC/laptop or browse them online.

They have advantages for anyone needing rapid access to a wide variety of published, copyright information.

eBooks can help your research by enabling you to bookmark chapters, annotate text and use instant searches to find specific words or phrases. Several eBook files would fit on even a small laptop or PDA.

NEW: Save money by eSubscribing: cheap, online access to any eBook for as long as you need it.

Annual subscription packages

We now offer special low-cost bulk subscriptions to packages of eBooks in certain subject areas. These are available to libraries or to individuals.

For more information please contact webmaster.ebooks@tandf.co.uk

We're continually developing the eBook concept, so keep up to date by visiting the website.

www.eBookstore.tandf.co.uk